THE CAMP DIRECTOR'S SURVIVAL GUIDE

Michael Jacobus

© 2016 Healthy Learning. All rights reserved. Printed in the United States.

No part of this book may be reproduced, stored in a retrieval system or transmitted, in any form or by any means, electronic, mechanical, photocopying, recording, or otherwise, without the prior permission of Healthy Learning.

ISBN: 978-1-60679-353-4
Library of Congress Control Number: 2016931496
Book layout: Cheery Sugabo
Cover design: Michael Jacobus
Front cover photo: Kyle Dreier / Chief Curiosity Director
kyle@dreier.com / www.dreier.com
709 2nd Avenue South, Nashville, TN 37210

Healthy Learning
P.O. Box 1828
Monterey, CA 93942
www.healthylearning.com

*"The world may be different
because I was important
in the life of a child."*

—*Forest E. Witcraft
(1894 - 1967)*

ACKNOWLEDGMENTS

It would be impossible to list the names of all the people who have touched my life along this journey or who have guided me through my many camp experiences, but those that stand out are listed on this page. Things they all have in common are their love of camp, the magic it creates in children, and their own high personal standards of trustworthiness & honor. Each one of them exemplifies the kind of person and camp professional I want to be.

- Bob Barram—Youth minister and camp director for the Piedmont Community Church and Camp Lodestar.
- James Jenner Jacobus—My dad. He sparked my interest in camping and was the finest Eagle Scout I have ever known.
- Jack Mead—My first ScoutMaster. Jack made me work for and earn everything I did. He always held me accountable.
- Billy Kennedy—The head counselor at Lodestar. The camp God of my youth.
- James Ferrigan—My co-conspirator in the revival of scouting units for our boys.
- Marshall Smith—My son's ScoutMaster. He gave them the same quality experiences that my ScoutMasters gave me. An excellent role model.
- Sloan Hamilton—She opened my eyes to the possibilities and reach of the greater camp community. Always there for me.
- Raina Baker—My guide as I became more involved in the American Camp Association.
- Michael Baum—Director of Camp Fox in San Diego and my jump-start inspiration to write this book.
- Tom Horner—Friend, leader, camp professional, and mentor, by example. Tom's career is an inspiration to many.
- Phil Lilienthal—Founder of Global Camps Africa. Phil gave me the life-changing opportunity to work at his camp in Soweto, South Africa.
- Michele Branconieer—Professional staff member with the ACA. If all camp professionals are like her, I'm home. I have arrived.
- John Van Dreese—A genuine leader who knows and lives the difference between leading & bossing. Thanks Victory!
- Tom Holland—ACA CEO, whose openness, creativity, & passion mirrors my own.

FOREWORD

I have always told camp professionals that they are just a little crazy to do what they do. After all, taking responsibility for the safety and well being of other people's children has got to be one of the riskiest tasks that an individual can undertake—ever! I also think that the enormity of that responsibility brings with it a certain kind of "lonely-at-the-top" experience that most people cannot imagine—unless they have done the job themselves. Individuals who are not in the field of camping are often mystified as to what a "camp person" actually does all year. After all, they think "camp happens" for anywhere from six to ten weeks in a summer. What else can you possibly be doing all year? The only other people who truly know what you face all year—not to mention what you encounter in the summer—are fellow camp directors. And they're just as crazy as you!

Enter Michael Jacobus. As someone who has been in camping for more than 30 years, both in the for-profit and not-for-profit realms, he is eminently qualified to offer the kind of practical wisdom that camp professionals can truly use. In The Camp Director's Survival Guide, Michael paints a rendition of the landscape that we all call camp, in a way that will put the smile of recognition on the face of every camp director who reads it. More importantly, he offers a kind of useful insight every camp director needs not just to survive, but to thrive.

To be successful as a camp director, you have be "your best self" with people who are often not returning the favor! When parents believe, lock, stock, and barrel, every word of their child's embellished version of an incident at camp, Michael's wisdom can come in very handy.

His "Think Like a Parent" session at camp conferences is extremely popular, and he serves up that wisdom in the first chapter of the book. The approach he calls "build it backwards," which echoes Steven Covey's maxim, "start with the end in mind," is a useful method that can be applied to a variety of situations, starting with the "How to Fire a Friend" scenario. As he says, firing a friend is one of the most challenging things you will ever do as a director.

But, hold on, the list never ends! When you agree to enter what I call "the white water of life" with families, as you do when you take other people's children and promise to return them safely and in an enhanced condition, you invariably encounter drama. Furthermore, let's not forget the fact that you work for nine months to get everything ready for your big "show," then hand it all over to a bunch of 18-to-20 year-olds, just as the curtain rises. As I said, a little crazy!

My favorite section of the book is the Case Studies section. Every director will think Michael was at your camp last summer! These are the situations that keep us up at night: the camper parent who calls in the fall with a situation of reportedly "near death" proportions that you were never aware of; the layers of poor judgment calls that staff make, when you have no idea of their existence; the morale problems that arise, even when you think you're doing the right thing.

It takes years to gain the depth of experience and the repertoire to be a truly competent, capable camp director. (Michael reminds us it can all be taken away in minutes. Please pass the Valium!) Reading this book, especially the chapter on how working in theatre prepares you for the "show" that camp is, will help shorten the trip. Happy reading and happy camping! And keep this book close by during the season. It just might help save you from disaster!

—Bob Ditter
Camp Consultant & Trainer

CONTENTS

Acknowledgments 4
Foreword (Bob Ditter) 5
Introduction 9

Chapter 1: Think Like a Parent 11
How many kids will your camp serve this year?

Chapter 2: Reputation 21
It takes years to build and minutes to lose

Chapter 3: On With the Show 33
How the business of camp is akin to theatre

Chapter 4: How to Fire a Friend 41
Saying goodbye to a member of your camp family

Chapter 5: Effective Facility Use 53
Thinking outside the box

Chapter 6: Engage the Nonprofit World 65
Even for-profit camps can benefit

Chapter 7: Volunteer Relations 73
How to combat analysis paralysis

Chapter 8: Case Studies 79
How to deal with challenging situations

Chapter 9: Closing Campfire 101
Final thoughts & resources

About the Author 106

INTRODUCTION

There are plenty of amazing resources available to help guide you through the nuts and bolts of how to run a camp. In fact, tips on an array of topics, including staff development, day-to-day operational challenges, effective food service, and health and wellness, as well as suggestions from several of the best programs that you can consider offering at your summer camp, are certainly not in short supply. Furthermore, countless books, educational sessions, retreats, and conferences have been designed to help members of the camp community, navigate the endless stream of options and concepts in order to create the perfect experience for both campers and staff.

Hopefully, The Camp Director's Survival Guide is a little bit different. While much of the information is applicable to any new camp professional, this book assumes that the reader is an experienced camp owner or director with a desire to go from good to great.

The genesis for this book started as a compilation of various sessions that I had been asked, or offered, to conduct at a variety of professional conferences and retreats. Most of the topics covered are a direct result of a situation arising and the need to find a workable option or an actual viable solution to that particular set of circumstances.

If this book communicates nothing else, I want you to take away and truly understand the huge responsibility and incredible honor it is to be entrusted with a child in a camp environment. No family dynamic, school atmosphere, or team community can compare to camp. The experience and friendships that occur at camp transcend and transform the lives of young people, campers and staff alike.

Those of us who have chosen to follow a career as a camp professional will tell you that we don't do it for the income … we do it for the outcome!

As a camp professional, you are among the chosen few. You have, within you, the ability to shape and guide the destiny of the next generation in an environment unlike any other.

Make it count!

1

Think Like A Parent

This chapter is based on a session that is typically attended by camp staff and program directors. On occasion, during this session, I will ask how many people in the room are parents. Unless there's someone a bit more seasoned (like from my generation) in the room, hardly ever does a hand go up.

One of my very favorite questions to ask in this atmosphere is: "How many kids will you have at camp this year?" This is any easy question to answer, or at least estimate, and usually attendees are eager to respond (bragging rights y'know).

More often that not, someone in the audience will ask me what I mean by my query. "How many per week? Or, do you mean the entire summer?" I then reply, "Just give me a number. Answer it any way you like." From there, I get numbers ranging from 50 to 800. All of the respondents are very proud of how many kids come to their respective camps.

I usually smile and tell them how awesome those numbers are, but in reality, they are all wrong. I then hold up one finger and tell them: You only have one kid in camp this summer … *MINE*.

How Do You Communicate Your Message?

The parent is your customer. Many camp directors will tell you that the camper is the customer, and the camper's experience is the driving force toward delivering a positive and profitable camp experience.

While that, of course, is true you need to think about the issue in a more appropriate, relevant way. For example, who selects the camp and compares it to others? Who pays for the registration fee of the camper? Who tells their friends and family about the good (or bad) camp experience? Who sends returning campers (and their friends) back to camp next year? The answer is straightforward… the parent.

This chapter is essentially about *SALES* and how effectively you communicate your camp message to your target customer. While it's directed toward the camp professional, I have found the strategies detailed in this chapter to be useful in a variety of business ventures, as well as in general life experiences.

Many camp directors get so caught up in the day-to-day operation of running camp that they don't spend much time thinking about marketing to the new customer. Returning campers tend to be a slam-dunk. Furthermore, if they have siblings, cousins, or friends, so much the better. What about the family, however, that has never heard of you or is new to the area or whose kids have just reached camper age? How does your camp stand out?

Your Online Presence

One of the first things that I tell camp owners and directors is to go visit their own website. I don't mean login or view it from the administration side. I mean pull it up from a web browser or smartphone and try to look at the site through the eyes of a parent who has never seen the site before.

I tell them to take notes—*LOTS* of notes. I even encourage them to make it a group effort and invite existing parent customers, staff, and family to do this exercise with them. What message is being conveyed by the site?

Is the website easy to navigate? Can parents obtain the information they need? Are their questions being answered? Not the answers you think they need, but the information they are really seeking.

As an example, I am always surprised by how many camps do not list their physical address on their home page. While it's on their camp map or directions page, and it's probably on their registration forms, in today's world of instant access and technological impatience, most parents want to look-it-up right now. One of their instant internal calculations will be based on where your camp is, how far away it is, how long a drive it requires, etc. More often than not, they then immediately gauge the costs associated with this particular option as a camp for their children, (both financially and in time commitment). The key issue is whether your target customer, the parent, find the information that they want in a user-friendly and quick way?

In contrast, I know of a camp website that has over 350 pages and links for parents to access information, the vast majority of which are completely irrelevant to the actual business of parent information and camper registration. The fundamental takeaway is not that you shouldn't have links to photo galleries, videos, and testimonials on your website, but you need to keep it simple. I recommend that you employ my personal rule of public speaking, or what I call the 3 Bs: Be correct – Be brief – Be seated.

Social Media

Do you know what is out there in cyberspace about you? Have you looked? In fact, venues in which information about you can be found exist, a list that includes Facebook, Instagram, Twitter, SnapChat, Yelp, parent groups, staff and alumni groups, The Better Business Bureau, and the Chamber of Commerce, as well as a multitude of online forums.

I don't mean *YOUR* page(s). I am referring to what others are saying about you and/or your facility. The "horror story" in my experience that immediately comes to mind is that of a camp staff's supposedly 'private', (or closed), Facebook Group page. That page contained photos of the camp staff essentially hazing each other by wrapping staffers up in duct tape (a *LOT* of duct tape). Well, as you might imagine, some parents of new staff saw this page.

Do you remember the campfire game called "operator"—the one in which all of the campers sit around the campfire, and the leader whispers a specific sentence or statement into the first camper's ear and from there the message gets sent around the circle? Remember how often the finished translation often sounded nothing at all like the original message?

Well, when this message was shared around the parent and community campfire, it went from something originally described as a fun team activity into a story of new staff hazing and abuse. Long story short, the police were notified, several staff were fired, and the story made the local paper. Understandably, it is not really the kind of press that you want for your camp.

This topic is something that most camps currently include in their staff trainings. I often cover the last part of the opening introduction to this book when I participate in a new training staff course. I try to let them know that their lives at this point are forever changed. They are no longer who they used to be. They are *camp staff!* They are real life heroes in the eyes of their campers, and as such, should now and forever, assume that role and live by that example, (both in-person and especially online).

So, go online, or ask friends to help, and very intentionally research your camp as a parent would. Find out what's out there!

Respond and Fix It

If you find negativity out in cyberspace, reach out to the person who posted it and try to address the matter. You may be surprised how far a small gesture will go. The worst thing you can do is to ignore the issue. While everything is not fixable, everything is certainly worth your attention.

Electronic Communication

How much is too much? This answer is different for every camp and every parent (or grandparent), dynamic. The best advice I can offer is to always be consistent.

I have found that the most well-received schedule of communication with your camp parent, will go something like the following:

❏ The Registration Process

Gather all the information you can. In addition to medical, dietary, and other health concerns, ask the campers about their summer plans outside of camp. Do they have siblings and/or pets? Is there any special information that their camp counselor should know? What previous camp experiences have they had and were they good or bad?

❏ Confirmation

We've received your registration, and we're excited you're coming! More than that, however, if a parent shared with you that a camper's birthday occurs during their camp session, acknowledge what you plan to do. Remember, you only have this ONE child in camp this summer.

❏ Pre-Camp

All of your pre-camp communication needs to make the parents feel that you have anticipated their questions and that you are looking out for the best interest of their child.

In the case of the returning camper, you'll find it very helpful to have notes from last summer's experience. Do you remember this camper? Do you have returning staff who worked with this camper last year?

More importantly, how you treat the family of a first-time camper will set the tone for the entire summer experience for that family. The parents of most first-time campers are very nervous. They may have unreasonable expectations, based on their own experiences when they were children and went to summer camp, and if they don't know you personally, you'll need to consider the source by which they found you. Did a friend refer them? Did they read your advertisement somewhere? Did they find you online?

Not every camp can do this undertaking, but one of the most impressive things I've seen done is the anticipation letter from the camp counselor. While this effort can also be an email, it needs to be handled in a very specific way.

The email, which should come from the camp director's email address, should contain the note from the counselor. This procedure will prevent parents from obtaining specific email addresses of individual camp staff.

Imagine being a parent who is sending their kid to camp for the first time and getting a letter like this, a month or so before the start of camp:

Dear Mrs. Smith,

My name is Paul Sanchez, and I will be Ryan's cabin counselor this summer. I just had a meeting with Mr. Jenkins, the camp director, and he shared with me some of the details of Ryan's registration form.

We are very excited that Ryan will be with us for his 11th birthday! With your permission, we'd like to make him "King of Camp" for that day. It's always a big deal, and I'm sure he'll love it.

I also wanted to let you know that I have been made aware of your concerns for him possibly being homesick. This is my third summer as a cabin counselor, and I have lots of experience making new campers feel safe and comfortable.

We can't wait to have Ryan join us in the Jedi Cabin this summer, and we'll make every effort to ensure that he has an awesome time.

Best regards,

Paul "Master Jedi" Sanchez

Just imagine the comfort-level that has just been created in the parent by receiving that letter. Think about the details featured in the letter. He knows *MY* son's name. He and the camp director had a conversation about *MY* child. They want to celebrate *MY* son's birthday at camp. He's already keen to *MY* concerns about homesickness.

How many kids are at your camp this summer again? – *BINGO!*

❑ During Camp

Parent communication during camp can be tricky. You need to make sure that you have pre-set policies in place for letters, care-packages, communication with parents and campers, and what to do in the event of an emergency or the occurrence of an unforeseen need to remove the child from camp.

It is usually desirable to have at least one means of communication from the camper to the parents and from the parent(s) to the camper during their stay. For camps that run multi-week sessions, a little bit more communication would obviously be expected.

The downside of care packages involves a situation when a parent sends unapproved items to the camper. This object could be candy or other food items, electronic devices, or other articles from your what-not-to-bring-to-camp list. The reverse is also true in the event of too much communication from the camper to the parent. For example, random homesickness easily becomes a daily tragedy, which, in turn, can result in electronic communication, such as text messaging phone calls and emails, becoming a crutch that impedes a successful camp experience.

Many camps employ a camp photographer. On occasion, this role is a dedicated position. Other times, it takes the form of extra duties assigned to a staff person at the time. Every time I've witnessed a camp with a photographer, the mission of the photographer is the same—to get at least one picture of every camper, smiling or laughing and having fun at a camp activity.

When these photos are shared with the parents, it becomes very difficult to get wrapped up in a homesick conversation or any sort of communication, in which the camper has told the parents they're not having a good time. The downside of camp photos is when you get the parent who wants to know why there are seven photos of camper-A, but only three photos of their child, camper-B.

Much like the letter from the cabin counselor prior to camp, I strongly recommend that your camp staff send a personal letter, note, or email to each camper's parents with some personal information about that camper's experience.

Make sure that all of your policies regarding communication are clearly detailed in your camp documentation, on your website, and in any communication you send to the parents before their child arrives at camp.

❑ After Camp

I am always amazed how little communication happens after the camp experience. These campers and their parents are your future customers, as well as your daily advertisement for next year's camp session. While I do not suggest any direct communication between your camp staff and their campers, I strongly encourage camp owners and directors to reach out at least twice between the moment that a camper leaves the camp at the end of the season to the pre-registration notification for next year.

A simple; "We enjoyed having you at camp this summer!" letter or card can be sent a few weeks after the camper has left camp. I've even heard of a camp that sends out communication at the end of the year and rather than making it a Christmas card or something seasonal, they suggest that the camper write a letter to his "future self," so that it can be shared at the camp the following summer. These types of communications keep the family engaged, keep them talking about camp, and keep summer camp in their family's planning mindset for the following year.

Targeted Marketing to Parents

Does your camp offer discounts for siblings? How about discounts or referrals or a "Bring-A-Friend" program? Do you have an alumni program, or some other vehicle in place to engage campers who are now adults as you market to their children?

The point to keep in mind is that there are a number of ways in which camps can achieve success in marketing directly or indirectly to parents. In this regard, being creative can be helpful. For example, do your campers leave with branded souvenir items or photographic takeaways of themselves and their favorite activity or their favorite counselor? Think about what you are putting in the hands of your campers to take home and 'advertise' your camp, while they're away from camp.

Straight Talk/Wildfire

One of the purposes of this chapter is to try to put you in the mindset of the parent—to anticipate their needs and desires, and to think about how they would like to be communicated with before the need arises.

In your advance communication, feel free to share any relevant good news or accolades about yourself, your staff, or your facility. If you have staff members who have gone to advanced training in specific activity areas or have earned degrees, by all means share that information. By that same token, you want to make sure that you clearly communicate to the parents that you will be responsive and attentive to any issue that comes up or any emergency that may happen.

On occasion, that means that you may have to take on a very uncomfortable situation. For example, I know of a camp that discovered a cabin counselor was smoking pot on his day off, and returning to camp in a somewhat altered state. This activity was in direct conflict with the camp policies (that get communicated to all parents), which are detailed in the staff manual. Rather than deal with that situation immediately and head-on, the camp owner's decision was to keep quiet and just get through the last few weeks of summer.

Long story short, the parents did eventually find out about that situation. The news spread like wildfire, and registration the following summer dropped by 40 percent. Furthermore, by the next season, that camp had shut down and remains out-of-business today.

The proper thing to do in that situation would have been to terminate the employee immediately and make arrangements for another staffer to be present in the cabin, so that the campers would have adequate supervision. The harder part then comes next. The camp owner should have personally contacted the parents of every camper in that cabin and informed them of the situation, assured them that their policies were being followed, and that their children were safe. It may have been a momentarily embarrassing and uncomfortable situation for that camp owner, but, in the long run, it would have communicated consistency and a level of comfort that the parents could trust and rely upon. No parent ever likes to find out about a distressing situation that involves their child, after-the-fact.

Custody

Many camps, these days, include verbiage in their registration forms that speak to child custody issues. For example, does the parent signing the child up for camp have authority to do so? Are there other parents, grandparents or guardians who also have a say, or worse yet, may show up at camp and claim custody of that child?

Have you ever had a noncustodial parent show up to camp, unannounced, with divorce decree papers in hand, insisting on taking the child away from camp? It isn't pretty.

Knowing it's a possibility will get you halfway towards resolving the matter.

As a camp director, I once had a noncustodial father show up at camp, demanding to take his daughter home. I had the camp nurse pull the registration documents for this camper, and the dad's name was not listed anywhere on the documentation. The approved pick-up adults were the camper's mother, her aunt, and her grandmother.

I apologized to the father and told him there was nothing I could do and that my first duty was the health and welfare of the camper. With no disrespect intended, I informed him that I didn't know who he was and that his photo ID and court paperwork by themselves did not authorize me to release the child to him. I then suggested that we call the nonemergency number for the local sheriff's office and have the deputy come out to the property. We also contacted the camper's mother to let her know what was going on and ask her for more details.

At the end of the day, the father was right. His divorce decree did allow him 50 percent custodial time with his daughter during school breaks. While chatting with the sheriff's deputy, the camper's mother confirmed those details. In essence, the mother had signed the camper up for a camp session that she was not authorized to approve.

Always try to put yourself in the position of the parents, and try to anticipate their wants and needs around their very genuine concern for the welfare of their child. Remember, to them, this young person is the *ONLY* child you have in camp.

2

Reputation

REPUTATION

[rep·u·ta·tion] noun

: the common opinion that people have about someone or something
: the way in which people think of someone or something

> *"It takes a lifetime to build a reputation and only 15 minutes to destroy it."*
>
> —Warren Buffett

With regard to the aforementioned, I feel that you should be asked certain questions. For example, did you read the definition of reputation? Do you understand what Warren Buffett said? Good! —then proceed to the next chapter.

But seriously, I am often flabbergasted by how little intentional effort is placed upon the reputation of the camp, the camp staff, the camp owners and directors, and the entire camp experience. One point cannot be overemphasized—your reputation is everything.

Much like the previous chapter, how you deal with issues and interact with the community around you will speak volumes, compared to whatever advertising you choose to put out there. It's easy to maintain a good reputation when everything is going great, when the campers are happy, when the food is good, and when families are signing up for next year. The real challenge occurs when there's difficulty, when there is bad publicity, or when there are uncomfortable hurdles to clear. How you and your camp staff respond to adversity will communicate a much clearer picture of who you are and your professional standards than just about anything else you'll encounter.

What is your reputation in the community? What is your camp's reputation? Do you even know? In fact, getting a general feel for how you and your facility are perceived within your community and across your target marketplace is very important information and will help guide you on what you should do next. It will also inform you if your image needs to be changed, modified, or supported.

Be Responsive

Businesses, in general, are very quick to jump on the bandwagon and respond to positive feedback. Favorable postings on social media tend to take on a life of their own. More often than not, multiple people comment on them, including, in this case, the owner of the camp property. In turn, a very positive conversation ensues. Conversely, an alarming number of companies, including camp properties, tend to ignore negative postings and negative feedback, believing that the problem will somehow magically just go away.

While I don't advocate taking on a full-time position of always falling on your sword and apologizing, when you encounter negative feedback or comments about a negative experience at your facility, you should immediately and very directly address the concern. An actual funny example of this situation was presented to a camp director in the form of a negative forum posting from a parent, who commented that their child was not allowed to participate in a campfire or have a s'more, while attending their camp program.

What made this situation funny was that the child was attending a day camp program and campfires only occurred with campers attending the overnight session. In this instance the camp director had three options. He could not respond at all, leaving the negative comment just hanging out there in cyberspace. He could respond truthfully and remind the parent that campfires and s'mores don't occur during day camp, but since nobody likes to be told they're wrong, (especially publicly), that probably wouldn't have gone over too well.

The third alternative for the camp director was to proactively and creatively address the situation. In this case, the camp director actually mailed a chocolate Hershey bar, a few graham crackers, and some marshmallows to the camper's home, along with an invitation to attend a campfire later that summer at no cost.

This tactic turned a negative situation into a positive experience for everyone involved. That parent has since told dozens of other parents in the area what a wonderful experience she had. Subsequently, many of those parents have signed their children up to attend future sessions at this camp.

- Cost to the camp: A little time, a few snacks and some postage.
- Benefit to the camp: A dozen new campers.
- Pretty simple math, huh?

Be Honest

It seems strange to even have to read the words, "be honest," but much like the example in the previous chapter concerning the cabin counselor who was smoking pot, how you communicate your intentions and how you are seen conducting yourself day-to-day, define who you are.

I've never met a camp director or camp owner who hasn't made a mistake. It may have been due to a complete oversight; the camp director may have assigned something to a member of the camp staff and it just didn't happen; or it might be due to any number of other factors. The point is that sometimes, things are going to go wrong. It's how you handle yourself, your staff, and the situation during these times that communicates to your customer exactly with whom they are dealing. Never forget that nothing creates distrust as much as being caught in a lie.

Own Who You Are and What You Do

Nobody likes to eat crow. The anticipation of owning up to a mistake, especially publicly, can have a paralyzing effect. It is so much easier to sweep it under the rug, pretend it didn't happen, and just move on.

Trust me, when you do something like that, your actions (or your choice of inaction) are noticed, known, and remembered in your community. Don't misunderstand, there's nothing wrong with taking a stand. Just make sure that the stand you take is consistent with who you are and the values you are trying to communicate that are associated with your camp.

Cultivate Allies

From a sales standpoint, it's certainly important to identify your competition. Perhaps even more important, is to identify other goods and services (from other vendors) that serve your target audience. For example, if the parent of the camper is your ultimate customer, in what other activities do they participate and what other businesses do they frequent for the benefit of their child, your camper?

An obvious alliance for a typical summer camp property might be the lifeguards at the county run beach, or the people who own the local horse stable. This factor is especially true if a camp offers those activities and doesn't specifically own the horses or have access to the beach on their property.

On the other hand, the issue involves more than just identifying other companies that you can use. Many camps reach out to every school in their geographic area that serves children within the target age of the summer camp. Chances are, your local schools know who you are and where you are and, at the very least, if there's a summer camp program at your facility. This knowledge is only the tip of the iceberg.

When I suggest that you cultivate allies, I want you to think about how you may be benefiting that school during the off-season. It's one thing to put up flyers that proclaim, "Come to Summer Camp!" at local schools or have the schools send the flyers home in the parent packets of every local student. It is quite another to offer that same school an opportunity to host an afterschool study hall or an afterschool Kid's Club that may have a camp theme on the school's property during the school year. The underlying point is that you need to adjust your thought process to a more global or at least a more community-minded position, and not simply focus on; "What's in it for me?"

Goodwill & Endorsements

Does your camp participate in any local fundraisers that benefit entities other than your camp? Such participation can be something as simple as having a couple of staff members wear a camp T-shirt and lending a hand at a car wash, a pancake breakfast, or at another local charity event.

Is your camp perceived as an active participant in the charitable functions of the local community? There is very little cost involved in sponsoring a local Little League team (especially, a team full of current and possible future campers), being the host location for a blood drive, or offering your facility as meeting space for the local Rotary Club or veterans group.

Reputation Repair Kit

When I conduct a session on this topic at a conference, the bulk of my time is spent on how to *FIX* a damaged or destroyed reputation. In that regard, the most important first step I always suggest is to… *OWN IT.* Even if, whatever it was had nothing to do with you, it's yours now.

The following example reinforces my point. I once took a position in Southern California as a program director. Wanting to connect with the community in a positive way, I reached out to all of the local agencies, such as the parks & recreation department, the local nature conservancy, the city council, and, of course, all of the local schools. Subsequently, I received a favorable response from all of them, except the parks department.

After three months of occasional emails and voicemails simply introducing myself and suggesting that it might be nice to connect (given that the park actually shared a property line with the camp where I was working), I finally received a reply. It came in the form of a phone call from the local ranger. He apologized that it had had taken him so long to get back to me, and that there had never really been good relations between the park and the camp. When I asked him the reason for the bad relations, he told me that the camp had put the county in a very awkward position by going outside their property line and creating easements in the designated open-space.

He continued to tell me that the parks department had contacted the camp management many times over the past few years and had been constantly blown off. Needless to say, the camp's reputation, at least in the eyes of this particular county agency, was horrific. I assured him that this was the first that I had heard of the situation, but that I would look into it immediately. I then asked him for details.

He agreed to come to my office, and when he did, he brought with him an aerial photomap of the camp and the surrounding park property. On it, he showed me the areas that the camp had created hiking trails that very specifically violated an ecological mitigation area. One trail went about a half mile off the property line of the camp and encroached into the protected open space.

He told me that the Army Corps of Engineers had brought up their concern about the trail going through the mitigation area and that the hiking trails that went out into the open space had placed the county park in violation of their easement agreement with the state authority for land usage. I then informed him we would discontinue using both of those trails immediately and shut them down with signs that said no access.

He thanked me, shook my hand, and left my office. I got a strong sense of a "yeah sure, I've been blown off before" kind of attitude and a "why should you be any different" message… loud and clear.

Later that afternoon, I met with my program staff and asked them about what goes on in these trails and why we use these trails. We determined that we could run the exact same programs with the exact same nature hike outcome and avoid using these areas. The next morning we had signs put up that clearly stated: "No Access." From that day forward, we discontinued using those trails.

Once the signs were in place, I took photos at both ends of each trail. The photos showed how we had closed off the trailhead and that we posted signs in all four areas, and had hung chain across each entrance, further indicating that the trail had been closed.

I then sent out a blast email to all my program staff and copied it to the park ranger. In it, I stated that the camp had been in violation of some land-use concerns pertaining to these two trails and from this point on, there would be no activity or access to either of those trails indefinitely.

As you might imagine, the park ranger quickly became my good buddy. Subsequently, we worked together on a variety of different issues over the course of a number of years. After that and to this day, the camp's reputation remains golden.

Everyone Wants to Be Heard

I probably say this phrase in every single staff training class that I teach. It doesn't matter if it's a camper, another staffer, a supervisor, a parent, a maintenance person, or a vendor. Everyone wants to be heard, especially if that person has something that they feel very strongly about or needs to be communicated.

In old-school sales training, you very often hear the phrase; "The customer is always right." When I do this kind of training, I say just the opposite. The customer is quite often wrong, but the customer is still the customer.

Furthermore, by customer, I mean anyone with whom you are communicating, the camper, the staff, the parents… anyone!

We've all been there. Very often the customer is dead wrong, but they believe they're right. Or worse yet, they know they're wrong, but they want to push the issue anyway, because they don't want to be the one who was wrong about the situation. They want you to be wrong.

Either way, listening is critical. You need to take in, listen, and absorb everything that customer is saying. First, you need to understand their concerns. Then, you need to communicate that they have been heard.

There isn't always an immediate solution. In reality, it's okay to say, "I don't know." It is not okay, however, to blow them off. If you need to research an issue that a customer has a problem with, give them a very specific expected time by which you will get back to them. If that time comes and you don't have an answer, you still need to contact them to at least to bring them up to speed on the status of your efforts.

While the aforementioned may all sound like sales training, it's really reputation training. As such, it all boils down to the Golden Rule: *Treat others the way you would want to be treated*.

It's OK to Apologize… Sorta

There's good quality customer service, and then there's overkill, with the possibility of falling on your sword unnecessarily. If you blew it, if one of your staff made a mistake, or if the camp made an error in someway, by all means, apologize. A sincere apology often goes a long way.

The underlying basis for the title of this section, including the word "sorta," is because you need to be very specific and thoughtful about exactly what it is for which you are offering an apology. In the overly litigious society in which we live in these days, you don't want a friendly apology to turn into an admission of guilt that gets used against you in some form of civil litigation.

"I'm sorry the kitchen served pizza two nights in a row," is a much different apology than, "I'm sorry your child didn't arrive at the airport for her first day of camp." This situation really occurred. The story about it can be found in Chapter 8, "Case Studies," detailed in the section, *WRONG PLANE*.

Obviously, how you handle any situation that would require an apology on your part will speak volumes about your reputation. Apologies that can be viewed as the assumption of guilt are something that you should run by your attorney or risk-management professional beforehand.

Act Immediately

On occasion, it's not so much what you do, but how you are seen doing it.

When it comes to your reputation, always imagine that you are being watched and that your actions matter. This factor is not something that you just need to be conscious about in the event of a complaint from a customer. Your staff is watching you, your peers are watching you, and even your campers notice how you behave. For example, do you deal with the situation immediately or do you blow it off? Do you respond when you say you will?

If you say that you don't know, but you'll find out, do you indeed find out and follow up on that topic with that person? The longer you allow time to pass before making a decision or being seen making a decision, just allows others to imagine their own reality of what you're doing during this time. I refer to this period as "dead space".

Think about anytime that you had to make a call to request some sort of customer service. The person you talk to on the phone says: "May I put you on hold?" Then you agree, and they do.

The longer you remain on hold, the more your mind runs wild. Why is it taking so long? Is my request really that difficult? What the heck are they doing?

Have you ever been unsatisfied with a phone conversation and asked to speak to a manager? That's a really uncomfortable situation, isn't it?

At that point, you tend to start thinking about what that customer's service representative is telling their manager about you. They weren't able to help you or give you a satisfactory answer, and now you've requested to escalate the situation over their head. Chances are that they're not super happy, and they may even have to explain themselves to their manager about why they were not able to resolve the situation. Oh yeah, you know they are now a really big fan of yours!

Keep in mind that same dynamic is happening when a staff member or a parent or some other person is waiting on you for information or for you to take action. How long are you going to make them wait? What's going through their mind about you and your camp, while you're making them wait? Perhaps most importantly, what will their mindset be once the matter is responded to or resolved?

I've had very upset parents be given an answer that they absolutely did not want, but the issue was researched thoroughly and quickly, and they were responded to in a clear and concise manner. They didn't leave happy with the results, but they did leave feeling that they have been professionally dealt with in an honest and responsive way.

Seek Help

This area is probably the one call-to-action that I really wish people would practice more often. The famous line written by English poet John Donne is "No man is an island," was true when he wrote it back in the 1500s, and it's true today. In reality a number of camp directors and camp owners get too wrapped up in their own ego and pride. As a result, they often fail to reach out for assistance, especially in complex matters. In fact, the most successful camp owners and directors I know are individuals who regularly network and communicate with their counterparts at other facilities.

Virtually all of the staff who have ever worked for me have heard me say, at one time or another, "Relax, it's just camp." I never say that with the intention of downplaying the importance of what we do. Personally, I believe that no one provides a camp experience better than my staff and I do. (Did you see that? That's where the camp director's ego comes in.)

I say it most often when being presented with something someone perceives as being a catastrophe or an emergency, that, upon mature reflection, may not actually be so. When I teach the session entitled, "Don't Panic," I cover a lot of issues for junior camp staff that they may perceive as emergencies that a more seasoned camp professional may have already dealt with a dozen times that summer.

There is certainly no shame in seeking help, and no dishonor in admitting you don't know something. Help often comes in the form of a friendly conversation with the camp director from another facility, who is willing to share with you their solution to a similar situation. Help can also be a conversation you may have with your attorney or your human resources specialist. You should also keep in mind that members of your camp staff can also quite often be a very helpful resource.

Lead by Example

Throughout my professional camp career, I have really enjoyed working with young people. One interesting factor that I came to realize, over the years, was that the young people I enjoyed working with, themselves kept getting older. Initially, as a teenage camp counselor, I really enjoyed working with the campers. Subsequently, when I became part of the program staff and eventually a program director, I really enjoyed working with the camp counselors.

In my role as an executive director, I have found that nothing really brings me greater satisfaction than seeing all of my staff, from the cabin counselors up to program directors, succeed, achieve, grow, and learn.

One of the most self-destructive behaviors that I've noticed among camp owners and directors is to be secretive or not include others (especially members of their administration team, in decisions that directly affect camp operations. While there may be quasi-legitimate reasons, on occasion, to not communicate all the details of a particular situation, in my experience, being open and forthright with your staff is critical.

One situation in which such openness might be exceptionally difficult to provide is for camp directors who work for larger corporations. Many corporate entities operate summer camp properties as part of their overall or annual programs. As such, the administrative person who oversees everything is usually not the physically onsite, summer camp director. The summer camp director may have other duties during the year, or may have been hired seasonally, just to run that camp. As a rule, seasonal staff are almost never included in conversations involving the annual bigger picture.

The first thing you have to do in your specific role, or in any position, is to identify the parameters of your knowledge and authority and get a very clear understanding of what you can and can't share with your staff.

As for whatever example you ultimately set, you might want to consider the following key issues:
- How do you live your life? How do you conduct yourself? More importantly, how would those around you answer these two questions?

How you conduct yourself, not only while working, but all of the time is noticed. We all build mental images and impressions of people in our lives, and those impressions get modified and adjusted at each new interaction. Your staff, clients and campers all have a mental image and expectation of who you are and whom they expect you to be.

So, who are you? Do you walk the walk?

3

On With the Show

Any camp staffer will tell you that camp is all about the performance! As a theatre-geek myself, I can attest to the fact that the efforts and skills needed to put on a successful performance, or a theatre season are the same talents needed to run a quality summer camp program.

To that end, I have borrowed the writings of my theatre-pal, Tom Vander Well, to offer a different way to look at how you run your camp. Note: *For those of you so inclined, Tom is a wise and prolific writer. He can be found online at:*

tomvanderwell.wordpress.com

Quiet backstage... the curtain is about to rise!

10 Ways Being a Theatre Major Prepared Me for Success
By Tom Vander Well (Jan 16, 2012)

❑ #1. Improvisation

The great thing about the stage is that when it's live, and you're up in front of that audience, anything can, and does, happen. Dropped lines, missed entrances, or malfunctioning props require you to improvise, while maintaining your cool. Theatre taught me how to focus, think quickly and make do, while giving the impression that you've got it all under control. It's served me well when clients, airlines, coworkers, or technology wreak unexpected havoc at the worst possible moment.

How many times have you had to wing it at camp? Being prepared for the unexpected should be routine for every camp professional. Giving your staff the authority to think on their feet and make decisions for the benefit of the camper, the program, and the property is key. If you don't train your staff in such a way that you trust them to do the job you hired them for, then you're probably in the wrong business.

❑ #2. Project Management

A stage production is basically a business project. You have teams of people making up one team, working to successfully accomplish a task on time, on budget, in such a way that you earn the applause and an occasional standing ovation. Being taught to stand at the helm of a theatrical production was a project management practicum.

A well-run summer camp has many leaders. From the admin team to the kitchen staff and from the janitorial & maintenance personnel to the staff who run your individual activity areas, every leader needs your support. Keep in mind that one of the quickest ways to demoralize your staff is to micromanage every aspect of what goes on at camp.

❑ #3. Working with a Limited Budget

Everybody who has worked on stage knows that it's not the road to fortune. Most plays, especially small community and college shows, are produced on a shoestring budget. This situation forces you to be imaginative, do more with less, and find creative ways to get the results you want, without spending money. Ask any corporate manager, and they'll tell you that this pretty much describes their job. Mine too.

Much like the theater analogy, I've never met anyone who has gone into the business of camp for the paycheck. This industry is about passion and delivering quality programs to campers. After all, we camp people don't do what we do for the income, we do it for the outcome. While different camps serve different demographics and range from nonprofit entities with almost no budget and a volunteer staff to what is generally referred to as a "rich-kid camp" with unlimited resources, the entire camp experience really boils down to the quality of the program.

❑ #4. Dealing With Very Different Human Beings

The theatrical community is a mash-up of interesting characters. It always has been that way. From fringe to freakish to frappucino-sipping socialites and everything in between, you're going to encounter the most amazing and stimulating cross section of humanity when you work in theatre.

In my business career, I have had the unique and challenging task of walking into the CEO's office in the morning to present our findings in an executive summary presentation and to receive a high-level grilling. I have then spent the afternoon presenting the same data to overworked, underpaid, cynical front-line employees only to get a very different grilling. Theatre taught me how to appreciate, understand, and effectively communicate with a widely diverse group of human beings.

The same factor holds true for the camp community. The staff you work with will have a variety of experiences and attitudes. The campers who come to your program will come from different backgrounds and bring with them their own unique perspective of the world. Also, don't forget their parents. Parents range from wealthy and entitled to some individuals who don't speak your language and have never seen green grass or a tree.

❑ #5. Understanding the Human Condition

Most people have the mistaken impression that acting is all about pretending and being "fake" in front of others. What I learned, as a theatre major, was that good actors learn the human condition intimately through observation and painfully detailed introspection. The better you understand the human being that you are portraying from the inside out, the better and more authentic your performance is going to be.

In my business, I am constantly using the same general methods to understand my clients and their customers, as well as myself and my co-workers. I believe that having a better understanding of myself and others has ultimately made me a better (though far from perfect) employee, consultant, employer, and ultimately friend. I didn't learn methods of observing and understanding others in macroeconomics. I learned it in Acting I & II.

As you and your staff interact with different personalities, you will discover the need to adapt your communication style. You may think you're being perfectly clear in the way that you communicate. Indeed, with some of your staff, campers or parents, your message may be coming across perfectly clear. Keep in mind, however, that other people with whom you interact are going to hear what you say very differently. What is crystal clear to one person may indeed be very confusing to another. As such, as a camp professional, it's your responsibility to make sure your message is clean and clear and delivered appropriately.

❏ #6. Doing Whatever Needs to Be Done

When you're a theatre major at a small liberal arts college, there is little room for specializing within your field. You have to learn to do it all. Light design, sound engineering, acting, directing, producing, marketing, PR, set design, set construction, ticket sales, budgeting, customer service, ushering, make-up, and costuming are all things I had to do as part of my college career. Within our merry band of theatre majors, we all had to learn every piece of a production, because at some point, we would be required to do what needed to be done.

I learned that I could capably do just about anything that I need to do. I may not love, it and I may not be gifted or excellent at it, but give me a task, and I'll figure it out. I now work for a small consulting firm that requires me to do a wide range of tasks. The experience, can-do attitude and indomitable spirit that I learned in the theatre have been essential to my success.

One of the best ways I've discovered to create and build positive staff morale is to lead by example and to show your staff that no job is beneath you. I try to leave my office at least once a day to tour the camp programs, in addition to being in the dining hall for at least one meal. This policy allows me to bond with my staff and be seen as someone other than just the camp director who is ensconced in his air-conditioned office.

Lending a hand and being seen participating in janitorial and maintenance duties, giving a lifeguard a break while you watch the pool for them, or assisting running the zip line or climbing wall, brings you to the same level as your staff and helps communicate the message that we are all here for the same purpose—a quality program to the campers we serve.

❑ #7. Hard Work

I remember creating a tree for one of our college shows. We had no idea how we were going to do it, but we made an amazing life-like tree that emerged from the stage and looked as if it disappeared into the ceiling above the theatre. My teammates and I cut out each and every leaf and individually hot-glued them to the branches of the tree. Thousands upon thousands upon thousands of them glued on, while standing precariously on a rickety ladder high enough above the stage that it would make an OSHA inspector soil his boxers. Sleepless nights, burnt fingers and a few brushes with tragedy were needed to get that tree done. But, we got it done. It was fabulous. A few days later, we tore it down, threw it out, and got ready for the next production. C'est la vie.

In business, I have periods of time with unbelievable workloads in which there are sleepless nights, seemingly endless days, and tireless work on projects that will be presented and then will be over. The report will be archived and I'm onto the next project. C'est la vie. I learned all about that as a theatre major.

Ask any busy camp director when they get time off, and they will probably laugh at you. Summer camp is a 24/7 job with very little downtime. Acknowledging that it is indeed hard work, even though it's fun, and letting your staff see that you are there going through it with them, creates that necessary teamwork bond and that shared feeling that we are all in this together.

❑ #8. Making Difficult Choices

You have got four parts and twenty-four schoolmates who auditioned. Some of them are your best friends and fellow theatre majors. Do you choose the inexperienced jock, because he's best for the part or the friend and fellow theatre major whom you fear will never talk to you again, if you don't cast him? I'm reminded of a project that was supposed to be performed outside in the amphitheater, but the weather was cold, windy, and miserable. Do I choose to stick with the plan, because it's what my actors are comfortable with, it's what we've rehearsed, and it will only stress out the cast and crew to change the venue at the last minute? Or, do I choose to think about the audience who will be more comfortable and might actually pay attention and appreciate the performance, if they are inside away from the cold, the wind, and possible rain? [I changed the venue].

Any businessperson will tell you that difficult decisions must sometimes be made. The higher the position, the harder the decisions, and the more people those decisions affect. Being a theatre major gave me a taste of what I would have to digest in my business career.

Tough choices come with the territory and are part of any administrator's job function. Camp directors are no different. For example, in that regard, Chapter 4, "How to Fire a Friend," explores some of the details related to the familiarity of camp staff and overcoming the difficulties when it's time to let one of them go.

Tough choices don't exclusively exist within hiring and firing practice, however. They occur in every area of camp. You may need to send the camper home or not accept their registration application in the first place. Telling parents that their child may not be the right fit for the type of camp you offer can be very challenging.

On occasion, a tough choice means turning away business, especially to a rental group that might mean considerable profit for your facility, if it doesn't quite fit with your stated mission. All too often, I have found myself using the term "We may not be the proper venue for your event or group."

A perfect example of this factor occurred when I was approached by a women's group requesting dates for what they called "a spiritual retreat." As it turned out, the group was focused on "... sexual, tantric healing, and personal exploration." Once they described their desire for "... raw, intertwined yoga, channeling the power of the sun" out on the main lawn, (translation = naked women, wrapped around each other on a warm sunny afternoon) my response was obvious. Since this event would likely be scheduled for a time when we would have several youth groups onsite, we went with the "We may not be the proper venue for your event" option.

❏ #9. Presentation Skills

Okay, it's a no-brainer, but any corporate employee can tell you horror stories of having to endure long training sessions or corporate presentations by boring, unprepared, incompetent, or just plain awful presenters. From what I've experienced, individuals who can stand up confidently in front of a group of people and capably, effectively communicate their message, while being motivating and a little entertaining, are among the rarest individuals in the business world. Being a theatre major helped me be one of them.

As the camp director, you are ON all day long. This factor applies to your camp staff, as well. Every minute of the day, everyone involved in the camper's experience, should be communicating the same message.

Perhaps, no corporation does this as well as the Walt Disney Company. Every employee with whom you come in contact at any Disney amusement park is trained to be on-stage the entire time. Anytime they can be seen or might come in contact with park guests, they are ON. It doesn't matter, if they are playing a beloved character or sweeping up trash,... all Disney employees are referred to as Cast Members because they are all critical pieces of the Disney puzzle.

❏ #10. Doing the Best You Can With What You've Got

Over the years, I've told countless front-line service reps that this is Rule #1 of customer service. You do the best you can with what you've got to work with. I remember an Acting I class in college, in which a pair of students got up to present a scene that they had prepared. They presented the scene on a bare stage, with no lighting, make-up, costumes, props, or set pieces. It was just two students acting out the script. It was one of those magic moments that happen with live theatre. The rest of the class was transfixed and pulled into the moment, reacting with surprising emotion to what they witnessed.

You don't need Broadway theatrics to create a magical theatrical moment on stage. You don't even need a stage. The same is true of customer service. You don't always need the latest technology, the best system, or the greatest whiz-bang doo-dads. A capable CSR doing the best they can and serving a customer with courtesy, empathy, friendliness, and a commitment to resolve can and does win customer satisfaction and loyalty.

Some of the most transformative moments in the life of the camper do not happen during regular program activities. They are more likely to occur in one-on-one settings with their camp counselor or their cabinmates, usually in their cabin or bunkhouse, or during meals or other quiet times at camp. Those life-changing moments and personal connections are what make camp such a special place.

One of the people I list on my acknowledgments page is Billy Kennedy, the head counselor at camp lodestar, the camp I called home for many of my childhood summers. Billy and I never developed a close friendship or really any friendship at all. He wasn't my cabin counselor, and being several years older than I, we didn't interact much at camp.

I acknowledge him in this instance because of what he did and who he showed me I could be. He was the leader. He set the tone. He directed all of the other staff on how to best connect with their campers and run the camp activities. Today, as an all-grown-up camp director myself, I have even that much more respect and admiration for Billy. He took ownership of his responsibilities and passed that authority along to his staff. Without conscious intention, he instilled in me the motivation, the work ethic, and the drive to deliver the best quality camp program possible.

Thanks Billy. You are *MY* camp hero!

4

How to Fire a Friend

This chapter is based on one of the worst (i.e., the most difficult to write) and most requested sessions I teach. How horrible the thought to fire a friend.

> The often-used description of this session reads as follows: *Camp staff dynamics include friends who are now supervisors and multi-year relationships that carry-on far beyond camp. Terminating employment of a camp-friend is akin to kicking a family member out of the house. In addition to detailing common best practices in this regard, this session explores ways to make a very difficult situation a bit smoother, including how to identify challenges, documentation methods, and possible methods for breaking the bad news. Done properly, this situation can be an excellent growth opportunity for everyone involved.*

Sounds great right? Oh my goodness, it's still one of the hardest things we camp directors have to do during the routine performance of our jobs.

In reality, the lead-up to termination of any staff, friend, or otherwise depends on your prep work and ongoing communication with your staff, especially as it relates to expectations and good documentation. This chapter covers some best practices with special attention to the inter-personal dynamic of the camp family environment.

There are a few different ways in which employees leave, including the following:
- They quit or resign.
- Their term of employment ends.
- They get laid-off.
- They get terminated.

Obviously, the first two are pretty easy to deal with. It's the terminations that pose personal, ethical, and possible legal challenges.

The Magic Wand—aka Build It Backwards

These are terms I use most often when planning a new event or contemplating the building of a new program or activity. Recently, I was discussing the concept of beginning a new science camp STEM program that involved taking high school students on daytime field trips (since high school students usually do not participate in overnight academic programs).

To a roomful of teachers, I said, "If you could wave a magic wand and have exactly the program and student experience you desire, what would that look like?" That is where the precept "Build It Backwards" begins. The same factor holds true for a variety of circumstances, including staff terminations.

A dear friend and camp mentor, James Ferrigan, often uses the phrase "Come with me in your mind's eye." At this point, I now invite you to do just that.

The staff person you needed to terminate has been let go. It went very smoothly, with no hard feelings. You both parted with, at best, good feelings about the situation, or, at the least, a civil discourse. How did you get there? —Build It Backwards.

"Build It Backwards" means that long before you have your termination conversation with the employee at issue, you do some homework. You need to physically sit down with pen and paper and write-out every detail that has led you to this decision.

Hopefully, approaching this situation in a thoughtful manner is something that you have become accustomed to and do on a regular basis. Good record-keeping and clean documentation are essential to good business practices and will eventually protect you in the long run.

When you "Build It Backwards," you are establishing a best-case scenario for the best possible final outcome. On the other hand, this strategy does not mean that you don't also need to plan for different variations of a termination event, including aggression, hostility, and anger. If you go through the steps in the proper order, however, you can minimize the likelihood of a termination becoming an ugly situation.

Accordingly, in reverse order (i.e., backwards), the following is how it should go:

- #7. The termination went well, and the staff person is gone.

- #6. You had a meeting with the employee (with one other senior staffer present), during which you went over the issues, discussed previous situations, and communicated that a decision to terminate had been made.

- #5. You conducted written and verbal reviews and/or warnings with the employee and clearly communicated job expectations and the company's discipline and termination procedures.

- #4. You and/or your designated staff took detailed notes and included dates, places, times, and other individuals present during any infractions.

- #3. You have an established policy in place that mandates that all employees get treated the same. No favoritism. The way you treat one is the way you treat all.

- #2. You had regular staff meetings, during which employee conduct and company policies and expectations were discussed.

- #1. You have shared a written staff manual, which includes employer expectations and reasons for terminations, with all members of the staff.

All of the aforementioned seems simple enough, right? Isn't that the way we all run our businesses? We all clearly communicate our company policies and our staff expectations, don't we? ... Sure we do!

The truth is that these business practices very often get blurred or completely overlooked within the familiarity of the camp family environment. This factor especially holds true with camp staff who return year after year, over a long period of time.

No matter where in the process you are, whether you have excellent record-keeping or none at all, it's not too late to start doing things right. I often suggest, with the attendees of my session on this topic, that they go back to their camps immediately after the conference and announce that they are establishing a new method for employee relations.

After all, don't we attend conferences for continued education and professional development? Aren't newly acquired best business practices something we would want to initiate immediately? Then, do so.

Given that we've now established the ideal order in which you would lead up to a termination of a staff member, let's start at the beginning and "build it forward" to get to that point:

❏ Staff Manual:

Does your camp have a document, or set of documents, that are shared with your staff that very clearly communicate expectations, and the methods of discipline and the procedures for staff termination? If not, you need to put something like that in place … immediately.

A staff manual should be a living document, subject to editing and revision on an annual basis, or more often as needed. Is yours up to date? Are your company policies very clear?

An earlier chapter, "Think Like a Parent," discussed the need for clear communication. You need to look at your staff manual from the standpoint of the newly hired employee. It doesn't matter if you think it's clear and easy to understand. You need to focus on whether the employee sees it that way as well. In this regard, I strongly recommend that you engage a third-party or perhaps a few people of different ages and different backgrounds to assist you.

Ambiguity in the document prepared by an employer tends to favor the employee. If an employee can claim that something was unclear or that they didn't understand a specific policy contained within your staff manual, by that time, it's usually too late for you to do anything about it.

❏ Staff Meetings:

Is your staff manual brought to staff meetings? Does your staff see it as a valuable reference document and refer to it regularly? It should, and they should. In reality, much of good business operations, especially when it comes to terminating an employee, rests on documentation, record-keeping and communication. If it feels like I'm repeating myself, I am.

My suggestion to everyone who reads this chapter is to go back to your office when you're done, pull out your staff manual, and go through it line by line to objectively determine if your communication is clear. If you feel it is, great. At a very minimum, your manual is probably due for a tune-up or an annual update. On the other hand, if you feel your staff manual and other documentation are not clear, or worse yet, does not exist, it's never too late to start.

After reading this chapter, it's time to announce a new beginning or fresh start with your staff. This situation is actually an opportunity to have them help you. I have found it very valuable to discuss with my staff exactly what they experience by being an employee of my camp.

I request that they share with me the good and the bad. I ask them to tell me what they think we should do differently. I solicit their input about the chain of command and supervisory communication. What could we do better?

This approach builds staff buy-in! You want everyone publicly onboard and in agreement with this "new and improved" process. You want to create a very clear set of guidelines and expectations (or polish up the ones you already have in place), so that all the members of your staff are on the same page. Even if you've been lax in the past, moving forward, you have to take great care to make sure that your policies are applied equally and fairly to every employee in every situation.

In this way, when you begin to experience difficulties with that 'camp friend' that you may have to terminate, you can begin to build the documentation paper-trail that will be used to support your decision when that day finally arrives.

Although this chapter does not specifically focus on sales training, there is a technique used quite often in car sales that I suggest you employ, when rolling out any new policy. It's called deferring to "higher authority." It's actually a way to block, for example, an aggressive car salesman who's pushing you to make a decision. When you respond, "I'll have to go home and discuss it with my spouse," that's deferring to "higher authority." It's really just another way of saying—"Hey, these aren't my rules."

Although they may really be your rules, your "higher authority" can be your attorney, your accountant, your board of directors, so on. You can communicate this fact to your staff by simply saying something like: "Gather round staff, we just completed an in-depth review of our policies and procedures. Upon review of the current labor laws of our state and after conferring with our corporate attorney, we are implementing some new employment policies."

Once you've established these policies and have gone through them with all of your staff, including all new hires, it becomes incumbent on you to live by them and run your business in the same manner. Getting back to the topic of, "How to Fire a Friend," you can bypass a lot of discomfort if you are very clear with those senior staff, long-time alumni staff, and anyone else, who may feel that the rules don't apply to them.

We all know exactly who those staffers are. They may be the children of important adults or donors. They may also be "connected" in a variety of other ways. They most assuredly feel entitled, like *this is their camp*.

One factor to keep in mind is that they might not even know that they behave like they do. It may be a situation in which a certain attitude has just been allowed to grow, because nobody ever broaches the subject, or was comfortable enough to do so, or quite honestly, even noticed. Now that you have new policies in place, it may be appropriate to sit down with those certain staff members and have a little bit of a reality check. In no way, does this effort need to be aggressive or take on the flavor of a punitive conversation. On the other hand, you really need to be clear and firm about how things may have been in the past and very definite about how things are going to be now and in the future.

This situation is a great time to ask if the staffer in question has specific concerns or for you to bring up specific behaviors, instances, or examples of any past behavior that may have been overlooked previously, which are now no longer acceptable. At the end of meeting or such a conversation, it's imperative that you both walk away with a clear understanding that a new day has dawned and a new situation exists and that all staff will be held to the same level of accountability.

New/Revised Policies

I know of a facility that offers year-round programming and, as such, allows a certain number of staff to live onsite. When a new camp director was hired, he commented, after touring the staff housing area, that it felt like visiting a frat-house. He said much of the original furniture was gone, replaced by personal furnishings from individual staff people.

There were no room assignments. In other words, staff moved into whatever room(s) they felt like. Some staff roomed together, while other staff insisted on having a private room. The only factor that they truly had in common was that nobody had any documentation. There was no housing agreement, no list of rules or expected behaviors, nothing.

What the camp owners didn't realize, and quite honestly were not paying attention to, was that each one of those staffers could have easily claimed the camp as their primary residence. In a way, they had squatter's rights.

Even if they had been terminated, they could have claimed that they lived on the camp property. Furthermore, they could also assert that even though their job was over, the camp was their personal physical residence. As such, had there been a termination of a member of that resident staff prior to any sort of housing agreement being in place, the camp administration would have found themselves very much like a landlord trying to evict a tenant.

One of the first steps that this camp director did upon arrival was to create a new policy for staff who lived onsite. This policy specified that it was a housing agreement, as opposed to a landlord-tenant agreement. Each member of the resident staff had to sign it in order to remain living onsite.

Most importantly, each housing agreement had a termination date. The termination date ended up being a three-month rotation, which is to say that the camp administration and the employee agreed that the employee could live there for three months. At the end of three months, there would be another meeting. The employee would then either be offered an opportunity to live onsite for an additional three months, or the individual's housing agreement would terminate.

In that way, the termination of the housing agreement was not a disciplinary function. It was nothing that the employee could act upon against the employer. It just became a simple business decision.

As camp professionals, most all of us know the feeling of dealing with a difficult staff person on a daily basis and thinking to ourselves: "If I can just make it until August." Oh, the magic of seasonal employment.

The housing contract just described is a great way to have that seasonal feeling with year-round employees. You can even expand that plan and create seasons within your annual calendar. For example, you can hire a lifeguard to work your spring season and employ that person from mid-March to mid-June. At the end of that season, you can then choose to offer that individual another season or let them go. Just like the previous housing example, this option simply allows for the employment season to come to an end.

Documentation

Documentation is extremely important. Frankly, it often amazes me how casually it gets treated sometimes. With regard to documentation, a good rule of thumb is: When in doubt, write it down.

Many times, I've had a camp staffer ask me if they should fill out an incident report for something that happened. Usually, the event involves an injury or other situation with a camper. On occasion, however, it deals with a staff member, or multiple staff members. As such, staff members are almost always the witnesses to an incident.

I answer the question of whether a staff member should complete an incident report the same way every time: "If you feel the need to ask if you should document a situation, via an incident report email or whatever, then you absolutely should." That little voice inside you that says, "Maybe I should write this down," or "Maybe I should tell someone about this," is almost always right.

Another key component to documentation, especially as it pertains to staff discipline, is consistency. Do you write up one staff member for a certain transgression that you let slide for another staff member? If that is your history, or if you have a habit of doing that, … stop now.

It is important to remember that staff favoritism will come back to bite you every time. If, for example, your waterfront or lifeguarding staff get special treatment, i.e., access or privileges that the rest of the staff do not, either those privileges need to be specifically spelled out as an expectation of that job description, or they need to be eliminated.

The situation in which documentation is particularly important arises most often in sexual harassment matters. There is almost no way to defend a claim that your company provided an atmosphere of acceptable misconduct, unless you keep meticulous records.

❑ Forms of Documentation:

Documentation doesn't always need to be a document. As such, you don't always need to hand the transgressing staff member a piece of paper. Very often, the first step towards documentation is a conversation or, more formally, a verbal warning. I actually have a discipline form that has boxes that you can check off for a written warning, a verbal warning, etc.

If I need to call a staff person into my office and give them a verbal or written warning, I always make sure to do my prep work and my homework. First, I make sure that I have all notes, witness statements, and any photos available. I also make sure to have reviewed those items with the appropriate people (be they the person who reported the incident or a secondary administration person). I want all of my ducks in a row beforehand.

Second, I never have any sort of staff disciplinary conversation alone, i.e., one-on-one. I always make sure to have a person in that second chair. The second chair person should never be equal or subordinate to the person getting the warning. The only exception that I've ever seen to that rule is a situation, for example, when the waterfront director is being disciplined, and there is no other senior staff person available. Then, you might choose another area director to be in the second chair.

While I never recommend having someone of equal status be in the second chair, some camp directors report that, on occasion, it was necessary, because time was a factor. In my opinion, I think that it's best to wait until you can find a more senior administrative person. If time is a factor for a verbal warning, you're probably doing it wrong.

❑ Discipline Form:

The form you use for written verbal warnings should be straightforward and simple. At a minimum, it should contain the following:
- The name of the employee and today's date
- The type of discipline it is (e.g., verbal, written, second written, termination, etc). If the discipline involves a specific incident, be sure to list a description of the incident, as well as the date and time it occurred.
- A list of everyone in the room during the discipline conversation (e.g., yourself, the staff member in question, and the person in your second chair)

As a rule, the discipline form should also include a few lines for notes or additional descriptions. In addition, the form needs to have an area for the employee to respond. This response typically entails an explanation or a retelling of the situation from a different viewpoint.

I always include a space on the form for corrective action, i.e., what must the employee do moving forward to avoid further discipline. There should be a signature line on the form to be signed by everyone in the room (again, the supervisor, the employee, and the person in the second chair). Finally, on the form there should be a space below the signature panel on the form for you to make notes, in the event the employee refuses to sign the document.

On occasion, an employee will refuse to sign a disciplinary document, under the false assumption that if they don't sign it, it didn't happen. Disciplinary documents should never require the employee to sign any sort of "confessing statement," acknowledging their misdeeds. The employee signature line is simply confirmation that they were present at the disciplinary meeting and that they received a copy of the document.

If they refuse to sign, they refuse to sign. Such a situation is why it's important to have that person in the second chair to also sign as a witness to the conversation that happened and to confirm that, yes indeed, the employee in question was present.

Termination Time

When the verbal and written warnings have failed, it's time to terminate. Hopefully, you've gotten to this point after making a painstaking effort to treat all of your staff the same, to not show any favoritism, and to clearly communicate your expectations and the consequences of failing to do so. It is also very important that you have all your reasons leading up to this termination clearly documented and witnessed. If you have done all of the aforementioned properly and in a conscientious business-like manner (with the exception of some kind of gross misconduct or criminal offense), you'll discover that most soon-to-be-terminated staff already know it's coming.

In a seasonal situation, you may have a few options. If you can make it to the end of the season and just be done with that staff person's employment, that may be your easiest route. It's always easier to let a previously agreed-to employment window close, than to terminate.

Assuming you don't have those options, you'll need to decide upon what manner of termination you want to move forward upon. Do you want to terminate this person and escort them off the property? Are you in a position to ask them to stick around and train their replacement? (This situation is very unique, but it does happen.) This scenario is another area in which you need to check with your human resources department and/or attorney. Most states require that you furnish a check for final wages to the employee who has been let go at the moment of termination.

Is this employee going to be eligible for unemployment insurance in your state? Again, this subject is something you need to educate yourself about and seek the advice of those professionals who are connected to your property and your business.

Before terminating any staff member, I always consider the "hit by a bus" question. If that individual was hit by a bus today, how do we get by? That's a somewhat crude way of asking myself what information do I need from them? What is their existing knowledge base? What conversations with new and existing customers are they currently engaged in? What property of the camp do they have in their possession or in their vehicle or at their home?

Another very important question that I think a lot of camp directors overlook is: "How will this affect the rest of the staff?" This issue is a biggie, especially in our industry. If the termination of the staff member (one of the camp family) is done improperly, it can have a devastating effect on staff morale and even cause other staff members to up and quit, either out of loyalty to that person or just in general protest.

Chances are other staff members already see this coming, too. How you, as a manager, handle it will either earn new and additional respect in the eyes of the remaining staff or cast you as the villain, as well as damage whatever respect that they had for you before this incident. *A bad manager can take a good staff and destroy it, causing the best employees to flee and the remainder to lose all motivation.*

During the Termination

Once the decision to terminate employment has been made, the actual termination meeting should be brief, dispassionate, and, of course, witnessed. You never want to get into long conversations with the terminated employee about specifics leading up to or the decision to terminate.

One important factor to realize is that a termination doesn't always mean that the employee has been fired. Sometimes, a decision to no longer continue the employment relationship (essentially a permanent lay-off) may be a better option for you. It certainly won't eliminate hurt feelings, but it often creates the ability for you to write a letter of recommendation, offer a severance of some sort, if you feel that's appropriate, or most importantly, obtain that staff member's cooperation as they transition off your team. The key phrase I stick to most in this situation is: "I understand that you may not agree, but the decision has been made."

During a recent staff termination, I actually had to say that line four times. It wasn't because I was trying to be a jerk. It was genuinely because the decision had been made, and there was no benefit to be gained from hashing out details or reliving the events that led up to the termination.

Think of it as a power outage. You're running your program, or you're working at your desk, and suddenly the power goes out. That is the decision. It has been made. The power is off.

Your terminated employee can gripe about being in the middle of something or not being able to see in the dark or that they have food in the fridge that's now going to go bad, because the power is out. None of that griping will magically make the power come back on. The power is out. The decision has been made.

Clean-Up

Once the decision has been made, and you have completed the termination, it's time to follow-up on what ever you've decided to do next.

Communicate with your staff immediately. You need to let your staff know that the terminated employee no longer works in your organization, and what that means for them in their position. Obviously, if the terminated employee was their supervisor, you'll need to reassure them and have the situation well thought out to ease any of their concerns.

This factor applies even to staff who wouldn't normally come in regular contact with the terminated employee. Staff also need to be communicated with so that they feel part of the team. Nothing makes a staff member feel marginalized more than learning about important news through the grapevine.

5

Effective Facility Use

Before we jump in and get too deep in this chapter, you need to make sure that you have identified what you can do versus what you want to do. In other words, if you are the owner of the property, and you are a for-profit enterprise, then you are likely relatively unrestricted in the ways that you use your facility. If, however, you are a nonprofit entity, or your camp is owned, operated, or overseen by a nonprofit group, there may be quite a few limitations on what you can and can't do.

For example, I know a camp facility in New Mexico that is owned by a nonprofit foundation. This property had discovered a way to make extra money during the off-season by hosting weddings. The county tax assessor did not view the for-profit wedding business as an appropriate use of a nonprofit facility. Long story short, the county assessed taxes on the square footage of the facilities that were used during weddings for that calendar year. Subsequently, the next January, that camp decided to no longer host weddings.

Before you go too far outside-the-box, be sure to check with your board of directors, local ordinances, and any applicable government agencies that may have a say in granting permission for what it is you want to do. Enough with the advance warnings, let's press on!

Maximize the Asset

Running a summer camp in the summer on a summer camp property is kind of a no-brainer, but what else are you doing with your property, either during the camp season, outside the camp season, or as a static stand-alone revenue-generator to bring additional income to your property?

Previously, in Chapter 2, "Reputation," the importance of being part of your local community and cultivating local allies was discussed. As such, the first thing you should do when you start thinking about creating additional revenue sources is research. Do your homework.

This factor is important for two reasons. You need to learn what else is out there (i.e., what other facilities and programs exist with whom you may be in competition?). Furthermore, you need to determine the needs of the community. Is there truly a need for an additional wedding venue, or is your community already saturated with that sort of thing? What do your local summer camp attendees, the kids who come to your program already, do in the off-season? The point is that you need to really learn the neighborhood before you can serve it.

Community Resource

Many camps have had great success becoming a community resource. For example, you can be such a resource by providing a meeting location for a local chamber of commerce group, becoming a local destination for a pumpkin patch, or serving as a Christmas tree lot. Camp properties can and should find a way to stay top-of-mind within the local community.

Education—Community & Academic

One of the hot topics within the camp community these days seems to be outdoor education. Everything, from week-long, resident science camp programs to half-day field trips, are allowing camps to tap in to this very profitable arena.

There are several factors that should be considered when contemplating adding an outdoor education program to your facility, including the following:

❑ Proximity of Schools:

Can your site be reached via school bus or private vehicle in a reasonable amount of time? This factor is relevant for several reasons. If a school group can't get to you and back within the regular schedule of the school day, then you are off the list for field-trip possibilities.

Distance is a bit less of a concern for resident camp programming. The concern of parents and their ability to get to their child in the event of an emergency, as well as your proximity to emergency services, are both concerns that you'll need to address.

❑ Staffing:

Many summer camps have no problem hiring staff for summer, but find it difficult to maintain a year-round team, especially when exploring the possibilities of adding new and untested programs. Beginning with a core group of volunteers and/or reaching out to the home school community may be a less costly way to get your feet wet. Camp alumni and recruiting from your local university or community colleges can also return favorable results.

❑ Program & Curriculum:

With the advent of the Next Generation Science Standards (NGSS), the science curriculum for elementary school children focuses more on the depth of a specific topic and less on the rote memorization of facts. There are many online resources for you to learn about the NGSS and how you can apply this curriculum to your program and facility.

This situation is one in which your relationship with the local academic community will be key. You need to do as much research as you can about what's available, as well as have a realistic understanding of what you can deliver at your camp. Most importantly, however, whatever curriculum you design needs to be something that the local academic community wants. It makes no sense to create curriculum and design a program in a vacuum that you then find out later does not meet the needs or desires of your targeted customer base.

❑ Be All Things…As Much as Possible:

If you decide to venture into academic programming, see if you can widen your reach and to touch as many program areas in a student's life as possible. This factor applies to the concept of being a community resource.

Why settle for just offering a fifth- or sixth-grade science camp program? Why not also try to capture that student during a second-grade field trip? Why not offer an end-of-the-year pool party for the entire school? Furthermore, as long as you're doing academic programming, why not offer STEM curriculum and a little bit of career & college readiness for those same students, when they reach high school age?

❑ Be Patient:

It's important to recognize that many schools who already embrace outdoor education and send their kids to science camp, most likely have a pre-existing relationship with another facility. Your task will be to sell them on why your camp is a better choice. What is it about your facility that makes it special? With regard to your programming efforts, it is also important that plan ahead at least a year or two in advance.

Remember Chapter 1, "Think Like A Parent." What makes your camp facility, staff, location, or programming more attractive to a camper's parent than someplace else? The key point is to find your niche, fill the void, and deliver that which is needed.

Rental Groups

I imagine that an entire book could be written for the camp industry about how to deal with rental groups. In this regard, the first point you need to determine is how much you're willing to let go of control of certain areas of your facility or, indeed, the entire facility. A rental group can be something as small as a local swim coach wanting to rent time in your pool for his private swim class to something as big as a nonprofit organization wanting to exclusively rent your entire facility for a week or more.

There are a lot of factors to consider when entering the rental-group business. In the first place, you should do some research in the landmark resource text, *ACA's Accreditation Standards for Camp Programs and Services*. There are accreditation standards that are specifically written for camps that serve rental groups. Those standards are put in place to protect the integrity of the program, as well as to protect you and your staff. They also address aspects of liability, which will help guide you through this area of potential legal landmines.

Once you've made the decision to accept rental groups, the first thing you should address is documentation. This situation is one in which you may want to budget some time and money to meet with an attorney and your insurance professional to determine where your risks are and how to create any necessary contracts and/or documents that protect you and your camp.

While it may sound a bit harsh, you have to assume that anyone renting your facility has never done so before, doesn't care at all about the property, and will likely be oblivious to your safety concerns. Furthermore, they will very often not communicate either those concerns or the specifics of your contract with their guests, staff, participants, and attendees.

In addition to whatever paperwork you have your rental group sign, it is very desirable to confirm with them what type of event that they're going to have on your property. Will they be bringing on third-party vendors, such as a food truck or a bounce house? If so, you should request proof of liability insurance (COI) from each individual entity, as well as a copy of their workers-comp policy, if they will be bringing their own employees to your site. With regard to workers comp, you should always verify coverage amounts and expiration dates.

Make sure that you include some sort of accountability for any damage caused by a rental group. It's usually wise to do a walk-through with the responsible party so that you're both on the same page, with regard to the condition of the property when they arrived. Factors like food service, alcohol, smoking, and supervision of guests (especially children) must also be addressed in your documentation.

Don't Become Their Event Coordinator

I have learned that rental groups very often have unrealistic expectations, especially when the person entering into the rental agreement is not the onsite point person during the event. If you don't want to spend the bulk of your time listening to the words: "miscommunication" or "misunderstanding," I strongly suggest that you conduct an on-paper, dry-run of any event for a rental group.

This step will save you hours and hours of headache and frustration. By dry-run, I mean exactly that. Schedule some time to sit down with your rental group representative (I suggest that you invite them to bring as many people with them as they want, so that all parties involved are on the same page) and literally go moment by moment through their event request.

Always start with preparation. Are any vendors arriving at your property in advance of the event? A list of possible purveyors, in this regard, would include florists, rental-party companies delivering tables and chairs, food deliveries, and any special staffing. What are the expectations of those vendors and your customer? Are these expectations in conflict in any way?

Do rooms need to be prepared in a special way? Are you having to create refrigerated or frozen space in your kitchen facility?' Is power a concern? Will they be bringing their own generators or plugging into your utility?

Once you've discussed all of the prep work, it's time to go minute-by-minute through the details of the event. Don't be afraid to overuse the word "expectations."

The following personal example can help reinforce the importance of addressing the issue of expectations. Once upon a springtime Saturday, we had two different rental groups at our facility. One was a church retreat for teenagers, having an event in the main dining hall, while the other was a corporate / company picnic kind of event, having their party out on the main lawn.

We failed to have the "expectations" conversation with either group. Imagine our surprise when the company picnic DJ began blasting music at the very same moment that quiet contemplation and testimony was being shared in the dining hall. Had we asked the proper questions to either group (or to both), we would have understood the church group's expectation and desire for peace and quiet outside the building during this time. We then could have tried to better juggle the schedule of the company picnic so that the DJ's time could've been put to better use. Lesson learned.

I can't encourage you enough to go step-by-step through the entire event and to have as much open dialogue and communication as possible with your client. This approach should eliminate, or at least greatly reduce, after-the-fact comments, such as, "We didn't know;" and "You didn't tell us" ... especially when it comes time to pay the bill, or worse yet, to pay for any cleaning or damage fees.

Always Cover Yourself

When all is said and done, you want to make sure that you personally, your staff, and your property are covered. If something bad happens at your property during a rental group's event, for example, a child gets injured, more likely than not, the news reports will not mention the rental group. Rather, the headline will be: "Child Injured at XYZ Camp!" As such, always confirm that your documentation and supervision are in place to make sure that such a headline doesn't appear.

Types of Rental Groups

Depending on the available space at your facility, and if you have the staff available to conform to specific needs, rental groups can be a huge benefit or huge headache or both. A list of several of the possible types of rental groups, along with several of their benefits and challenges, includes the following:

❑ Church Groups:

As a rule, these are very easy groups to have as rental clients. For the most part, the church group events are well-planned and very program-driven, especially given the amount of time that they have scheduled to be onsite.

One challenge that I've noticed with church groups is that, typically, a church group reservation does not require a lot of program staff. Having been a camp staffer myself as a young person, I'm always on the lookout for what's best for the property, best for the customer, and best for my staff.

An area director with whom I once worked told me that it was hard to get excited when a church group was scheduled to be onsite, when "all they ever do is eat sleep and pray." That was a direct reference to the fact that when you have this type of rental group on your property, very often you are not paying lifeguards, shooting-activity staff, or climbing-activity staff.

Furthermore, depending on the budget of the church group, they may or may not want to take advantage of your camp's meal service. I have worked with groups that didn't really have budget concerns, and they wanted every minute of the day planned and scheduled. As such, they paid for all of their meals. I've also worked with some very financially challenged groups that wanted to bring their own food onsite, as well as sleep on the floor, on bedrolls, or in their designated meeting rooms, because they just couldn't afford our standard accommodation rates.

❏ Pool Renters:

Pool renters are a seemingly easy rental group. When I first got involved with pool rental groups, it was mostly because having an aquatic facility sit empty and unused for any length of time made me itch. Subsequently, the biggest challenge I discovered with pool rental groups is supervision.

Typically, a pool facility located on a camp property is much different than that of a community pool at a city recreation center. We have actually had to incorporate verbiage into our pool-rental contract that mandates that an employee or a volunteer of the pool-rental entity needs be present to literally stand guard at the entrance gate and check people in and check people out. This mandate became a necessity when we found unsupervised minors roaming the property. In this instance, by roaming, I am referring to the fact that once the pool class had ended, some of these kids took it upon themselves to leave the pool area and go look for the parent who is supposedly coming to pick them up.

If that child was no longer on the pool deck when class was over, and the swim coach was done locking up, the coach had no reason to stay. He believed that all of his swimmers had gone. We even ended up having to require one group, whose participants and parents vary frequently, to hire one of our camp staff employees to be on-guard at the gate and run check-in and check-out procedures for their swimmers and their families.

Another difficulty that you'll encounter with renting your pool facility, or indeed any part of your facility, is the retail expectations of the client. For example, the water in our pool is 80° every day of the year, year-round. One day, when a rental swim team arrived, the pool was 72°. The entire team was out on the lawn, doing push-ups and sit-ups, because the pool was just too cold for swim practice.

Side note: I grew up learning to swim in Lake Tahoe, where the average water temperature is around 60°. As such, a 72° pool is like bathwater to me, but this isn't about MY perception, expectation, and understanding, now is it?

Remember what was said about communication, contracts, and facilities being understandable and acceptable to you … versus being understandable and acceptable to your customer? As such, maintaining your facilities in a market-ready, retail-rentable condition is something every customer is going to expect, and something you'll have to seriously consider the costs of, before jumping into the rental business.

❏ Exclusive-Use Groups

One of the most profitable types of groups we rent to are those requiring "exclusive use" of our facility. Exclusive use means just that. This group wants the entire property to themselves and does not want any other group onsite when they are present.

To determine what to charge a group, on a per-day basis, for exclusive use of your facility, you will need to account for a few key indicators. If, for example, you were to individually rent out every rentable facility on your camp property, what would you charge for each area? The total of all of those numbers would be your starting point for a base day-use fee for an exclusive use rental group.

Other factors should certainly be taken into the consideration as well, things like the group's intended use of the facility, what other facilities in your area might charge for similar events, and your relationship with the customer. With regard to this last factor, you need to ascertain the client's intentions. Is this going to be a one-time use event, or is this customer planning on coming back year after year, wanting to do this event again?

Another point to consider is whether this group truly needs exclusivity, or could they get by with something more like a "primary use / first choice option"-kind of reservation? Primary use is another alternative that I have found that works very well with rental-group customers. Not only is it often less expensive for them, it also allows me to have other people onsite, so long as the other groups don't interfere with the primary group.

When we rent to a primary use group, we go through the same steps that we go through with any regular reservation. We walk them through a day-by-day, hour-by-hour plan of their event. If we discover, for example, that their event won't go anywhere near the zip line or the climbing wall, then I may ask permission to have other groups use those facilities, as long as they don't interfere with the plans of the primary users or take up any parking spaces that the primary users may need. On occasion I even guarantee they won't even be seen.

❑ Food Service & Renting Out Your Kitchen:

At this point, I need to take a moment to apologize to any camp cook, kitchen director, or food & beverage manager, because I'm about to suggest ways to enhance camp revenue by renting out your kitchen. What I really want to write is: "Don't ever do it! Understand? Good! Let's move on."

Sadly, however, we reside in reality-land. As such, you will sometimes get those exclusive or primary clients who want to prepare their own food. On occasion, this desire is because they have special menus, which can include religious foods that your kitchen is not prepared to serve. More often than not, however, it's due to a cost factor. For example, they may have volunteers who want to donate their time to help prepare the food. Perhaps, there is a vendor that is willing to donate food to their group. In reality, a variety of other factors could be affecting their desire to prepare their own food.

As with any other part of your facility, renting out your kitchen for someone else to use should be well thought out because it carries considerable risk.

The risk of something getting damaged, of food handling not being done properly or of the staff / volunteers getting injured is very real. And, the list goes on.

I have rented out my kitchen facility a number of times and have found each experience to be a new learning opportunity. I believe I have finally hit upon the right way to do it. It should be noted, however, that just because what I'm about to describe works for me, does not necessarily mean that it will work for you.

When I'm writing an exclusive-use or a primary-use reservation contract, I do not include food service or access to the kitchen as part of the deal. Those conversations are separate and include separate agreements and fees, primarily because food service is expensive. Even though it is a critical component of any user's event, it sometimes is not a top-of-mind detail with the people with whom you may be working to arrange this reservation.

If a rental group wants to rent the kitchen and prepare their own food, the following are the additional hoops that we require them to go through:
- We charge an additional flat-fee of $500 per day for kitchen access.
- We require that one of our kitchen staff be present at all times. Although this person can volunteer to assist the rental group (and often does), their primary function is to safeguard the camp property and make sure that it's used properly.
- If the rental group requires dry-goods, refrigeration, or frozen storage, we will try to clear out our products and/or store them in such a way that it is a very clear that this is our stuff over here, and those empty shelves over there are for their use.

The additional challenge we have discovered, in this regard, is that we will often have the need to serve meals on the day of departure of the rental group, or, certainly, on the day after they leave. This situation requires us to accept food deliveries and have our kitchen staff in a position to be prepped and ready to go when the next group arrives.

Renting the kitchen can also create an issue with your staff. If you are running a year-round facility, or if you have program groups onsite during the time before an exclusive-use group arrives and during the time after they leave, handing over the kitchen, in essence, creates an unplanned and often unpaid vacation for your kitchen staff.

All of the aforementioned really boils down to how badly you need the additional revenue and what are you willing to do to generate that outside-the-box business?

6

Engage the Nonprofit World

Whenever I get a room full of for-profit camp owners together, I always ask them about their involvement with nonprofit groups and foundations. Most of them will tell me that because they are a for-profit camp, their pricing structure usually puts them out of reach for nonprofit events. I will also ask them if they've taken advantage of any nonprofit fundraising to send kids to their camps. Invariably, they will all say no, because they believe they don't qualify because they are not a nonprofit camp. Not true. At this point, before I go any further in this chapter, I'm going to strongly suggest that you speak with your board of directors, other owners or shareholders, your accountant, and your tax attorney. In no way am I an expert in any of these areas. This book is meant to share ideas and open your eyes to possibilities, not create directives of steps that you should undertake without exercising your own due diligence and checking with your own experts.

For-profit entities, including camps, can indeed benefit from the nonprofit world. There are just very specific ways you need to go about it, and very specific things you cannot do. Overall, however, there is no reason you can't benefit in some of the same ways a nonprofit entity benefits.

Establish or Connect With a Foundation

A for-profit camp that, does this amazingly well is Camp Kennolyn in Northern California (www.kennolyncamps.com). Kennolyn is an amazing summer camp facility, very well run by an outstanding and dedicated team of professionals. If I could go back in time to when my (now full-grown) children were little, I'd send them to Kennolyn for summer camp. It's everything a summer camp experience should be.

While Kennolyn is a for-profit enterprise, the family responsible for the founding of the camp has created a nonprofit foundation (www.caldwellfoundation.org). The mission of the Caldwell Foundation is to send kids to camp. That's it.

Right now, as you're reading this book, you could go to the foundation website and apply for a campership to send your child to any camp you choose. The fact that camperships, through this nonprofit foundation, can be awarded to send kids to for-profit camps, is just an added benefit for the for-profit camp, in this case Kennolyn.

Can I make a tax-deductible donation to Camp Kennolyn? No. Can I make a tax-deductible donation to the Caldwell Foundation, which will ultimately benefit Camp Kennolyn? Yes. Simple, huh?

Establish a Core Group of Volunteers

I know of dozens of camps, both for-profit and nonprofit, that have created or inherited a core group of dedicated volunteers (many of whom are camp alumni), who dedicate time, treasure, and talent to the ongoing success of that camp facility. Several of these individuals have even started their own non-profit foundations, for the specific purpose of supporting the camp entity and its programs. The underlying point is that you should never underestimate the passion, drive, or dedication of a volunteer. Previously, in Chapter 2, "Reputation," Warren Buffett's famous line about building your reputation and how quickly you can damage it was discussed. Keep in mind that a truly involved and engaged volunteer can be better than gold for your camp, as well as your reputation. Volunteer relations will be covered in more depth in the next chapter.

Donate Time, Fees, & Programs to Nonprofits

Before I go any further in this chapter, let me again clearly and strongly emphasize the need for you to consult your tax attorney and accountant on all of the concepts detailed in this chapter before implementing any of them. For example, you may find it quite beneficial to market your camp to nonprofit groups (especially, if you have slow-time or downtime that you need to fill) at a free or reduced rate, thereby creating a tax deduction / donation event.

Many nonprofit entities that want to have program opportunities at your camp go through their own grant application and fundraising procedures. Much like the Caldwell Foundation, those funds get raised for the benefit of the nonprofit entity. If that nonprofit entity chooses to use those funds to come to your camp, and if you can make your camp attractive by lowering your rates, while still generating at least a modest profit, it becomes a win-win for both sides.

Warning—Avoid Loophole Temptations

There are indeed a great many pitfalls and challenges running a for-profit camp in a largely non-profit world. The following example clearly illustrates why it's critically important to make sure that you are involving your account and tax attorney.

A for-profit camp was taking advantage of a tax credit offered to organized camps. The way the credit was worded, it allowed for an exemption of the payment of occupancy tax for kids attending a summer camp program. The camp in question chose to stretch that exemption and began listing wedding attendees and other overnight guests (individuals from retail reservations) as "campers." When tax-season rolled around, and they reported 12,600 summer camp nights (an average of 200 kids per week for a 9-week summer), but over 27,000 camper nights for the total year (all without paying ANY state occupancy tax), they got hit pretty hard with penalties and fines.

That camp had several other problematic issues with their employment practices, including the hiring of unqualified "friends," the questionable practice of extending benefits to extended family members, who were living out-of-state and had no connection to the real-world operations of the camp, and engaging in some improper quid pro quo with camp vendors. Because of these, as well as a variety of other, less-than-above-board business practices, that camp is no longer in business.

Become Nonprofit

Today, many camps are choosing to obtain nonprofit status. Either the entire corporate entity is becoming a nonprofit or just the camp property is achieving its own status as a stand-alone nonprofit entity. In reality, the effort seems to be a growing trend.

There are many things to consider before converting your organization from for-profit to nonprofit. In that regard, among the pros and cons, courtesy of the experts at www.grantspace.org are the following:

❑ Pro:
- Tax exemption/deduction. Organizations that qualify as public charities under Internal Revenue Code 501(c)(3) are eligible for federal exemption from payment of corporate income tax. Once exempt from this tax, the nonprofit will usually be exempt from similar state and local taxes. If an organization has obtained 501(c)(3) tax-exempt status, an individual or company's charitable contributions to this entity are tax-deductible. There are a variety of non-profit structural options under the Internal Revenue Code. Check with your accounting, tax, and legal professionals to help you "Build It Backwards" to determine which structure is best for your organization.
- Eligibility for public and private grants. Nonprofit organizations are allowed to solicit charitable donations from the public. Many foundations and government agencies limit their grants to public charities. A helpful tip in this regard is to be absolutely clear and transparent when accepting donated funds for specific (or non-specific) purposes.
- Formal structure. A nonprofit organization exists as a legal entity in its own right and separately from its founder(s). Incorporation puts the nonprofit's mission and structure above the personal interests of individuals associated with it. While this regulation is great for personal liability protection, not always great for the control-minded individual.
- Limited liability. Under the law, creditors and courts are limited to the assets of the nonprofit organization. The founders, directors, members, and employees are not personally liable for the nonprofit's debts. There are exceptions, however. For example, a person cannot use the corporation to shield illegal or irresponsible acts on their part. Also, directors have a fiduciary responsibility. If they do not perform their jobs in the nonprofit's best interests, and the nonprofit is harmed, they can be held liable. This factor is something to keep top-of-mind at all times, with regard to all of your official actions as a non-profit.

❑ Con:
- Cost. Creating a nonprofit organization takes time, effort, and money. Because a nonprofit organization is a legal entity under federal, state, and local laws, the use of an attorney, accountant, or other professional may well prove necessary. Aside from legal or other consultant fees, applying for a federal tax exemption can cost $500 - $1000 or more, in addition to state fees for incorporation. All factors

considered, creating the proper structure, articles of incorporation, etc. are well worth the financial investment to get it done right.

- Paperwork. As an exempt corporation, a nonprofit must keep detailed records and submit annual filings to the state and IRS by stated deadlines, in order to reatin its active and exempt status. No detail is too small or exempt from scrutiny. If you choose the non-profit route, be prepared for lots of paperwork.
- Shared control. Although the people who create nonprofits like to shape and control their creations, personal control is limited. A nonprofit organization is subject to laws and regulations, including its own articles of incorporation and bylaws. In some states, a nonprofit is required to have several directors, who in turn are the only people allowed to elect or appoint the officers who determine policy. How you form your entity will have permanent repercussions on how you are allowed to operate. Pay special attention to how you want to structure your board(s) of directors. The next chapter discusses analysis paralysis and what can happen to a top-heavy, often overly self-important board, and how their actions can actually work against the best interests of the organization.
- Scrutiny by the public. A nonprofit is dedicated to the public interest. As a result, its finances are open to public inspection. As such, the public may obtain copies of a nonprofit organization's state and federal filings to learn about employee salaries and other expenditures. If you take this plunge, be ready to live in the world of full fiscal disclosure.

The decision to convert from for-profit to nonprofit status involves more than simply filing to become tax-exempt. Initially, becoming a nonprofit public entity will require you to consider whether your current business activities would actually qualify as charitable activities under section 501(c)(3) of the Internal Revenue Code (IRC).

Since you will ultimately need to change your filing status with the IRS, it is important to research their regulations on charitable organizations. Keep in mind that the IRS classifies other types of tax-exempt entities, such as business leagues, labor groups, and social welfare organizations, each with their own restrictions and eligibility requirements. You will also need to check with your state agency (typically, the secretary of state or attorney general's office) to find out what required filings you might need to submit. You should also contact your state's charity office and discuss your situation with them.

- One last thought. While most states do not prohibit an entities' Executive Director or other paid staff members from serving on their organization's governing board, this type of arrangement could lead to conflicts of interest stemming from the board's role in oversight. Since the board is responsible for evaluating the performance of key staff, it would be a direct conflict of interest for an executive director to participate in board decisions about employee performance and compensation, particularly their own. It would also be difficult for the executive director to make impartial decisions relating to such issues as staff cuts, budget allocations, and changes to program.

Excluding the executive director from board service, however, does not mean that they can't attend board meetings. Executive directors can and should be part of important board discussions. They are, after all, likely to be the most well-informed individual in the organization when it comes to understanding the mission, programs, and finances of the nonprofit. In that regard, it can be good practice to include the executive director as an ex-officio or non-voting member of the board, so that this individual may participate in board meetings but still avoid the appearance of any conflicts of interest.

In instances in which the executive director might still have a seat on the board, it's important to have an effective conflict-of-interest policy. This policy should state when it is necessary for any board member, including the executive director, to recuse themselves from certain votes or discussions in which a conflict of interest may exist.

7

Volunteer Relations

For the purposes of this chapter, the word 'volunteer' does not refer to a teenager looking for service hours or helpful parents volunteering to stuff your camp Christmas cards into envelopes.

The most beneficial and sometimes frustrating person to deal with is the volunteer board member, a committee chairperson, or a volunteer who is a former staffer, alumni or benefactor. I have no doubt that these types of volunteers mean well. They quite often have the very best of intentions and will tell you to your face that their only interest is the success of your camp.

How they view that success and how they define it, however, is often another matter entirely. Many of these individuals have a very specific and narrow viewpoint of what the success of your camp looks like. Their perception is often based on their own personal experiences, the time they spent volunteering for other companies or groups, and how much of their personal ego is wrapped up in their act of volunteering. If they have donated money and/or have their name attached to a building or other manifestation of recognition, you may want to buckle-up!

Much like setting the stage with your staff by creating a clear and concise staff manual and building your reputation on the fact that you will behave the same way every time in every situation, you need to also create a similar atmosphere with your volunteers. On occasion, a volunteer can be your boss. Very often, the CEO of a nonprofit must answer to a volunteer board of directors. Sometimes, a volunteer might have a connection to your property that you don't know anything about. They may also have a local business or political connection. Take lots of notes, and always thank volunteers for their time and their input. Being able to identify exactly where the power is and who has a personal stake or ego connected to their volunteerism will serve you well.

By nature, I'm not a very patient guy. As such, waiting for a committee of volunteers to make a decision is one of those things that drives me crazy. One of the best lines I've ever heard about committees is: *A camel is a horse designed by a committee*. So true.

Analysis Paralysis

Volunteer boards and committees often suffer from analysis paralysis, or the inability to come to a final, conclusive decision. This situation can be crazy frustrating for the camp director, especially if you're waiting for that decision so you can take action.

One of my favorite authors on this topic is my friend Jeff Boss. He is a former Navy Seal, who currently offers his special brand of talent and experience as an executive & leadership coach. He has graciously permitted me to share his special brand of wisdom with all of you. You can find him online at: www.adaptabilitycoach.com. I've researched and written much on this topic, but I've come to think that Jeff says it best with his relatively short list of five factors to consider, when attempting to overcome the "analysis paralysis" of decision-making.

Nobody likes being wrong. The need to feel valued is an intrinsic human desire that manifests itself through the choices we make and how we communicate those choices to others. When it comes to making a decision, it's natural to want to be "right." After all, making the wrong statement or otherwise contributing in a wrongful way is about as fun as failing at a competitive sport (remember Martina Navratilova's quote: "whoever said, 'it's not whether you win or lose that counts,' probably lost.").

Decision-making is similar insofar as the choices you make are a reflection of the values, beliefs, morals, and intentions that not only shape your behavior, but also identify you as a person, as well impact others. What, then, do you do in today's world, where there is so much information to navigate? After all, trying to stay up to date with the latest viewpoints and updates is akin to the human version of an information hamster wheel: you can run along it all day, but never actually arrive anywhere. Rather, it's up to you to decide when to stop.

To help avoid the pitfalls of analysis paralysis, Jeff Boss detailed the five following considerations to keep in mind when inundated with so many bright, shiny balls of info:

❑ Set a Drop-Dead Date:

In today's interconnected world, nobody makes decisions in a vacuum. In other words, the decisions made by one leader can have vertical and horizontal effects that are both internal and external to the organization. As such, if people or departments are waiting on you, then progress is at a stalemate. Determine the last possible timeframe by which a decision must either be made or removed from the decision-making table.

❑ Get a Sanity Check:

Including others in the decision making process serves multiple purposes. First, it shares your thought process as a leader and, thus, serves as a coaching tool for up-and-comers. After all, what leader doesn't want to improve their people? (Well, the toxic ones, that's who) Second, you build diversity of thought that affords you greater context that only adds to your decision-making repertoire for next time. While I'm neither advocating a democratic leadership style by any means, nor condoning one either, leadership is, in fact, situational. Obviously, you can't enlist alternative viewpoints all the time (e.g., when time is of the essence), but when you can, it only serves the effectiveness of the outcome.

❑ Curb Your Curiosity:

One of the culprits contributing to analysis paralysis are details, specifically, the desire to excavate deeper and deeper every new detail that arrives on scene. To satiate the intellectual curiosity that yearns for more information (and therefore stalls progress), set parameters for yourself concerning what you need to know (now) and what you'd like to know (in the future). If the information you currently have addresses your needs, it's time to move forward.

❑ Recognize That Moons Will Never Align:

No matter how much information you have, there will always be more information available (somewhere). Decisions will never be optimal for this very reason—ever. There are, however, optimal moments during which decisions can be made. Remember, just because you arrive at one conclusion doesn't mean that you can never adapt to a new one.

❑ Stair Step to Your Decision:

Rather than looking at the decision to be made as a one-time, main event, consider smaller, yet actionable, decisions that can be made now or that lead up to the main one. Even just the tiniest shift of momentum can have a positive snowball effect that wriggles you out of the paralysis associated with making the "perfect" decision.

In the military, it doesn't matter in which direction you choose to move when under a mortar attack, just so long as you move. Decisions are never final for the simple fact that change is never absolute. Rather, change is ongoing. To stay competitive and progress at the rate of change requires adaptive decisions that can be iterated and improved upon on the fly.

—Jeff Boss

If you have these challenges with your volunteers, I strongly suggest that you share this book with them after you've read it. Much in the same way that I suggested you announce to your staff that from this moment forward you will be implementing new policies, revising your staff manual, and holding everyone accountable to the same level of expectations, I encourage you to share the information in this book, especially the chapter on volunteer relations, with those volunteers you think would benefit from it the most.

Keep Them Involved—Ask for Input

Not all interactions with volunteers are negative. In fact, volunteers can be an amazing resource. Chances are that they have vastly different experiences and a much different skill set than you.

You should develop a routine of keeping your volunteers in the loop, especially those individuals who sit on any boards or committees that may affect the way you are able to do your job. I also suggest that you reach out and communicate with key volunteers during times when you don't need anything, just to check-in. If a volunteer feels that they only hear from you in times of need, they may begin to lose interest.

Don't Wing-it/Respect Their Time

When arranging for a team of volunteers to help at your facility, or if you have a base group from which to choose, always have a plan. Many a volunteer has become frustrated or disenchanted by offering their time, after being told that their help is needed and appreciated, only to have nothing to do on the planned day. I've always found it better to be open and honest with volunteers about exactly what's needed and what everyone's expectations will be.

Keep in mind that it is in your best interest to plan any sizable project for which you will take advantage of volunteer labor or assistance. Decide before the job begins, how many man-hours will reasonably be needed and be very clear about the physical requirements needed by the volunteers.

We once had a group of 40 men volunteer for a 6-hour, "work-detail" one day. Our site manager and program director had projects and tools ready and waiting. When this group arrived, 15 of the men were senior citizens, with a variety of mobility issues. In fact, two were in wheelchairs, with their portable oxygen tanks in tow. When the group leader asked me if we had an air-conditioned space for the less-mobile volunteers, I knew there had been a communication error.

Never forget: Nobody plans to fail… they fail to plan.

8

Case Studies

In the course of compiling information and session notes for this book, it occurred to me that I should probably include some real-life, real-world case study information. For that purpose, I reached out to the camp community and asked several owners and directors, if they would be willing to share some of their experiences.

As such, this chapter includes an assortment of stories, each featuring one or more of the various challenges we have encountered in our professional camp careers and what solutions we were able to find.

> *Disclaimer:* As they used to say during the intro of the old TV cop-show, *Dragnet* ... The stories you are about to read are true. The names have been changed to protect the innocent, and the guilty, and occasionally, the stupid.

Concussion Test

An 11-year-old, male camper (let's call him Josh) was one of those always "bouncing-off-the-walls"-type of kids. He was having difficulty keeping his focus and staying with his assigned group. One afternoon, he was running up a grassy hill and not paying particular attention to where he was going. When he came up over the last berm, he collided, full-speed, into another young man who was running back, looking for him. They both fell to the ground. Josh got hit in the mouth when he impacted against the other boy's forehead. Josh had a split lip and likely bit his tongue in the crash, while the other boy received a small gash on his forehead and needed a Band-Aid, as well as requiring an ice pack.

This incident was described, days later, by his mother, after hearing a much modified and exaggerated account of the incident by Josh, as: *"Josh was run into by another boy, knocked unconscious and left unattended for almost two hours ... with a mouthful of blood."* That last part is my favorite; "... left unattended for almost two hours, with a mouthful of blood." Yep. That's just how we roll here at Camp Crybaby.

Anyway, back in the real-world, Josh and the other boy got up, and the camp nurse treated their injuries. She checked-in with both boys during the rest of the day, and everything was fine. Both boys said they were okay and showed no signs of greater or more serious injury the rest of the day.

That night, as is customary, I had my staff do their usual camper wellness checks. In a nutshell, that's when each camper personally speaks to their cabin counselor and confirms how they are feeling. We decided that it wasn't enough to simply check on the ones complaining of homesickness or showing signs of mild dehydration. We now check-in with every camper, every night, even if it's simply to ask; "How was your day?"

The cabin counselor assigned to Josh's cabin was a 23-year-old named Andrew. This was Andrew's second season at the camp and apart from having a little too much ego once in a while (I'm sure that no one reading this chapter has ever encountered that sort of problem before, right?), he had never really had a disciplinary incident.

On this particular evening, while doing a wellness check of all of the campers in his group, he asked Josh how he was feeling. Josh replied that he had a little bit of a headache, but that it was nothing to worry about, and that he felt fine.

Andrew, in an effort to lighten the mood and not so much with the intent of performing any sort of medical diagnosis, raised his index finger in front of Josh and exclaimed, "Follow my finger with your eyes." By all accounts, it was a playful exchange, Josh and Andrew were both laughing about it, and Josh was sent to bed.

The next morning, the right side of Josh's face and cheek appeared bruised. Josh became very worried. Not that his injury was worse than anyone previously had realized, but that his mother would see the bruise and be very upset. Apparently, there was quite a family story about the need to always be careful with Josh, given his mom's, arguably, overdiligence at checking him for scratches and scrapes and bruises, almost on a daily basis. While we had the feeling there was more to the story, we didn't pry.

Josh was part of an academic science camp program. As such, a few of his teachers were present during the camp. One of the teachers had called Josh's mom and explained to her what had happened. She told her that she didn't feel there was a need for Josh to go home and that Josh was doing fine. His mother chose not to come and pick him up early. It should be noted that as an added bonus and fun fact, Josh's mother is an administrative assistant at the Los Angeles office of the FBI, while his dad just happens to be a sergeant with the LAPD.

The next morning was the last day of camp. Josh got on the bus and went home with the rest of the kids from school. His mother, upon seeing the bruising around his face and listening to Josh's enhanced version of events, Including the; "I was left unattended and unconscious, with a mouthful of blood for two hours" story, claims to have taken Josh to urgent care later that evening.

Although no examination record was ever shared with us at the camp, Josh's mother stated that the attending physician at the urgent care offices told her that Josh had quite possibly suffered a concussion in the camp collision. She was also especially upset noting that the camp staff must have been aware of the seriousness of his injury, because Josh described having undergone a concussion test. Obviously, Josh had described to his mother what his cabin counselor had done with his "follow my finger" test in the cabin.

Lesson: Make sure that your staff fully understands what they are and are not authorized to do. Only your designated health officer should be conducting anything that could even remotely be viewed as a medical procedure or diagnostic test.

Concussion Test – Part II (The Solution)

One little tidbit not mentioned previously in this story was that Josh was on "strike #2" of our behavioral guidelines and pretty close to being sent home anyway. Of course, those disciplinary issues did not come up in the light of the victimization his mother felt he had received at the hands of our camp staff.

At any rate, Josh's parents asked if they could meet with the camp staff that was in charge of supervising their son. We did arrange an opportunity for them to meet with the two primary cabin counselors and to review the recordkeeping of the camp's health officer for that week of camp.

The mutually agreed upon solution was to put those two cabin counselors on probation and restrict them from overnight camper supervision, until such time that we could schedule a refresher staff training course. We invited Josh's parents to attend part of that training, so that they could speak from a parent's viewpoint to all of the camp staff about just how important it is when a parent entrusts you with their child. As a result, what turned out to be a potentially devastating situation ended up with full buy-in from the parents and actually having them appear as guest speakers for the next staff training.

Lesson: Right or wrong, parents want to feel heard. Make sure to address any concerns and complaints head-on and in a timely manner. You may also be surprised at how much people are willing to help you and your camp, simply because you are humble and ask them to share their concerns and/or experiences.

Denied Medication

Anyone who has attended one of my "Think Like a Parent" sessions recently has had the pleasure of listening to one specific voicemail message that I once received from an upset parent. I had to learn how to edit the sound file to bleep out the last name and the phone number, but otherwise it's a perfect example of what happens with incorrect or limited communication.

The situation involved having a young man arrive for a weekend camp (Thursday to Sunday), bringing with him his migraine medication, to be taken as needed. Thursday afternoon (the first day of the camp program camp), he told his cabin counselor that he had a headache, whereupon he was escorted to the health center.

At the health center, he was asked if he was suffering from a migraine and offered some of his medication. He declined, stating that it wasn't a migraine, and that he was just really tired. He was then allowed to lie down in the health center and was given lots of water. We even brought dinner from the dining hall to him, because he was still saying how tired he was at mealtime.

The camp nurse called home and left a voice-mail, stating that he was in the health center complaining of a headache (not a migraine), and feeling tired. After dinner, he joined the rest of the campers for the evening program and was about to attend the opening campfire, when his dad arrived to take him home (apparently after hearing the message left by the camp nurse). The camp nurse communicated that he seemed fine and would certainly do well if he was allowed to stay for the camp weekend. He was taken home anyway.

Fast-forward <u>three weeks later</u>, when I get the following voice-mail from his mom:

> *Hello. My name is _____ and I have a son who attended your camp a few weeks ago. He arrived on a Thursday, with his medication. Staff were informed that he gets severe migraines.*
>
> *He went down to one of your counselors with a migraine, and they made him sit in an office for an hour and a half, telling him that he could not call me. I would appreciate a phone call back, my number is _____. My name is _____, and my son's name is _____.*
>
> *I ended up picking him up the first night of camp with a migraine. He ended up throwing up all day the next day. He was sick for three days.*
>
> *I just want to know what kind of a policy it is that you guys have that you tell the children that they're not allowed to call if they're sick and to leave him sitting in a room for an hour and a half, when everyone else is having dinner.*
>
> *I'm very disappointed with the way that this matter was handled. I would appreciate it if you could please call me back, and I can explain the situation to you more in detail.*

I called her back immediately and told her that I had no knowledge of her son being in the health center three weeks earlier. Typically, I get copies of "incident reports," which are generated for serious injuries or for any event that requires a child to be sent home. I do not get reports on campers who are simply tired and are in need of a little water and a rest break.

I told his mother that I would find out the details she was referring to and call her back right away. She replied, "Oh sure, you're going to call me back. Yeah, right."

I promised her that I would call her back within 60 minutes, and if I did not, she was welcome to call me on my personal cell phone, for which I gave her the number. (Remember Chapters 1 and 2, "Think Like a Parent" and "Reputation" respectively.)

I then immediately met with the camp nurse to discuss this camper and asked to see her logbook. It was meticulous and incredible. She had made notations of every time that he had been offered and refused medication, as well as every time that water was given to him and the instance when a meal was delivered to him.

When I called the mother back, I literally read her line-by-line the entries from the logbook. There was a long moment of silence on the phone, and then she said three words, "That little shit."

I immediately reassured her that I was sure that her son told her the details as he remembered them (so, don't go kill him just yet). I also confirmed the fact that our first priority was the health and wellness of our campers.

Lesson: Keep very detailed, impeccable records. Medication dispensing, first-aid, incident reports, everything!

Lice, Lice Baby

One summer, I worked as the program director for camp with a very long history and family tradition. More than half of the campers who came to this camp every summer were from what were referred to as "alumni families." In other words, the same kids or their family members had come in previous years. Very often, the parents of these campers had come when they were children. On occasion, even their grandparents had attended this camp as campers.

I must say that I noticed a certain relaxed or "old-school" attitude toward policies and procedures existed during my time at this camp. I was assured, however, that their ways were tried and true and not to worry.

Other camps I have worked at did medication check-in and a health screening of every camper upon arrival. The atmosphere of this camp was very casual. Although medications got turned in, they very often were not double-checked or even itemized very well.

Camper health screenings were also extremely casual. I even felt a sense of insult from a few campers, as if we were accusing them of carrying the plague or some other such low-class infection. Many of the campers had arrived for multiple-week sessions. As such, the general attitude was to have them go through a health screening within the first few days of arriving camp. No big rush.

On day three of the current camp session, the two international campers (twin sisters from France) underwent their health screening. Both girls had lice. Because it was now day #3, they had already spent two nights in their cabin with other campers and their cabin counselor.

Needless to say, everything in that cabin needed to be treated, washed, and sometimes treated again. Every other camper in that cabin had to be checked, preventatively shampooed, or treated for their new infection.

When their parents, who were back home in France, were finally contacted, they responded, "Oh dear. We thought that we had taken care of that problem before they left." In other words, they knew the whole time and did not communicate it to the camp!

Lesson: Always health screen your campers upon arrival at camp. Don't trust any documentation that arrives with them. Always check for yourself.

Layers of Mistakes

The first layer of bad decision-making occurs when a counselor is showing off for his group at archery. Because he didn't do a proper arrow check, he failed to notice the arrow he was about to use was splintering about halfway down its wooden shaft.

He proceeded to load it and give it an "impressive" draw. When he released it, a chunk of the arrow shaft broke off and got lodged in the loose section of skin that bridges between his thumb and his forefinger. Although it was only about a half an inch long, it was completely inside his hand and very painful.

He arranged coverage for his group and came down to the office for first aid. We don't have a camp nurse, but we make sure that at least one staff member is an EMT.

The second layer of bad decision-making occurred with the EMT thinking that they would be able to fish the chunk of wood out of his hand with a pair of tweezers. Needless to say, the counselor was drenched in sweat and writhing in agony, as the EMT poked and prodded into the nerves surrounding the chunk of wood. The hand has lots of nerves.

After about 10 minutes of writhing and futile prodding, I called a halt to the ad hoc surgery, and we took the counselor to an emergency room for proper care. The upside of the situation is that other counselors learned from this mistake to pay closer attention to the soundness of the archery equipment. Furthermore, medically, we now always err on the side of caution and take anything the slightest bit unusual to an emergency room and treat only the most superficial injuries ourselves.

Lesson: Safety should always be top-of-mind with your staff either when they are onsite at your facility, or representing your camp in any way.

Staff Morale

A few summers ago, I found myself short-staffed because of late dropouts (this situation was due to some lower-than-normal numbers in the odd weeks of the summer, as well as our summer program director having her baby 10 weeks premature). Right in the middle of summer, there was an incident that changed staff morale for the remaining four weeks.

After three incredible weeks of camp, anticipating an extra day off, some of our staff members decided to take to celebrating a little earlier than they should have. It had always been our camp policy that "While kids are in camp, there shall be no drinking of alcohol on campus."

Obviously, that policy is in place in the event of any emergencies and to prevent the chance of any campers seeing or hearing a "party." Counselors, most being under 21 anyway, had no issues with this rule, particularly since they sleep in dorm rooms in the same hallways as campers. Program staff, i.e., older instructors, are allowed to leave camp, if they are not working that night, and go into town to enjoy some time off.

Kitchen and maintenance staff live in onsite housing around campus. We have always had an understanding that they could have a beverage or two in the comforts of their house. We have found that because those men and women were adults and did not interact with the kids at night, this soft policy has never been a problem.

After the night program came to a close, some of the program staff attended a small birthday celebration in a kitchen staffer's housing unit. This housing area happened to be in the middle of campus, right next to the main camp office. The party was quiet, and while I assumed some drinking was occurring, I did not worry, given that it was late and non-disruptive.

Counseling staff is off at 11 p.m. Once all of the campers have been asleep for some time, the counselors can leave the dorms. Two people always remain on-duty and must stay in the dorms. Everyone else must return to sleep in their own bed.

At around 11:45 p.m., the party started to increase in noise and attendance. I happened to be up late working, getting things ready for the long weekend off and making sure that all work was done for departure day.

At 12:30 a.m., I realized that it was time to put on my "director's hat" and put an end to the party. Upon entering the residence, I observed nine staff members (three counselors, five program staff, and the kitchen staffer whose residence it was). One of the program staff happened to be the assistant program director, who was filling in for the absent program director, who had had her baby prematurely. Everyone was drinking. I told them all that the party was over, to go to bed, and that we'd resolve the issue in the morning.

To give you a quick update on the structure of leadership, I am the summer camp director, in charge of the counseling staff. There is a program director, a kitchen director, and a maintenance director. We all report to the camp/facility director, who then reports to the executive director.

The next morning, I spoke with the camp director and we started to make a plan with the ED and our HR department. My position was that we should fire everyone involved and send a message to the rest of the staff, thus gaining full credibility as directors. The camp director thought we'd be too short-staffed if we did and that we should only fire the counselors, since they are younger and should have been in the dorms with the kids. Since this day was a departure day for kids, it would have been easiest to fire everyone and tell them they needed to be gone by Sunday morning, when the new kids arrived.

After numerous meetings and back and forth, it was decided that no one would be fired, and that we would simply not ask any of those staff members back the following year.

As you can imagine, the staff morale quickly went out the door. People knew they could break the rules and get away with it. My morale went out the door, as well. How was I to manage a staff who couldn't respect me?

The remaining four weeks dragged on and on. Finally, it came time for the internal, end-of-summer evaluations. With my three staff members, it was easy … they would not be asked back the next summer. Two of them understood, but the third one, who happened to be the kitchen director's niece, was furious. I questioned her as to why she was angry.

Come to find out that the program staff members were never told that they'd be asked to not come back. In fact, they were all told they had jobs the following summer. In fact, the assistant program director was to be promoted to the program director.

As you can imagine, the off-season came, and many of our staff members complained and eventually decided not to return. These were some of our best staff. Because of this situation, however, they did not want to work with rule breakers.

We learned from this situation, however. We made our rules clear in training week—"No drinking in camp, while kids are in camp!" Eventually, we decided that it would be best to ask those staff members involved not to return. As directors, we came up with clear policies and procedures, if this situation were to occur again.

It doesn't matter if we're short-staffed. Better to be down a few staff members than to have a full staff who isn't emotionally in it.

Lesson: Don't feel scared to fire anyone. It sends a message. Your A+ staff members will continue to come back, and your staff members who feel they can get away with things will be asked to leave. Morale will be at its highest.

Romeo and Juliet

We'd been having ongoing problems that were centered on the romantic relationships of some of our staff. During this one week, however, when we had a few different rental groups on the property, the situation came to a head.

One visiting group leader asked me, "Are they a couple?", while gesturing over to a pair of my staff. Apparently, they were being a bit too cozy with each other in public.

Later that same day, a different adult from a different group, motioned to a different pair of my camp staff and asked, "Lover's quarrel?" In this instance, an obviously upset female staffer was stomping away from her male staffer boyfriend, in a very loud manner.

I found this instance to be very troublesome, because we devote considerable time during staff training on the topic of how the staff is to present themselves, comport themselves and in every way act in a professional manner, including the issue of possible staff romance. We actually have a very specifically worded, written policy that discourages staff romance and outlines the policies and procedures around such a relationship.

Reading it, you can tell a lawyer wrote it. Basically, it says that while we recognize personal relationships can develop, especially among staff working in close proximity in a resident camp environment, the forming of romantic relationships is strongly discouraged. It goes on to say that any staff member who is engaged in a relationship that creates a distraction to themselves, the other party involved, any other members of the staff, or any camper or guest, will be offered relocation to a lateral staff position at another facility.

Finally, it states that there is no guarantee that a lateral position at another facility will be available. In short, it's a very polite and politically correct way of saying, "Do this, and you're fired."

My solution to the situation was to send an email to the program director that was also blind-copied to all staff members known to be in romantic relationships, in this case six people (three couples). The email, however, stated that if you were one of the 10 people receiving it, you have been identified as being in a staff relationship. The relationship policy had been cut and pasted into the email along with a very stern directive that this email would be their only and final warning. It also noted that from that moment forward, anyone found to be engaged in a romantic relationship with another staff person, such that it was brought to the attention of other staff campers or guests, would be immediately terminated.

Lesson: Always have crystal clear written policies that your staff reads, acknowledges, and signs. Also, make sure they receive a copy.

Wrong Plane

On occasion, I consult with a company that runs weeklong, academic programs on university campuses during summer. As such, they have student-campers sign up from all over the country and travel to those campuses, sometimes by airplane.

One camp director shared with me a particular story, in which a young man got on the plane and flew to the wrong state to attend one of these academic programs. The process in place for arriving campers is for the staff to meet the plane at the arrival gate. Very often, there is advance documentation of the camper's arrival, because the students traveling are minors, and their parents need to give the camp staff permission to go through security and meet the unattended traveling minor.

In this instance, when his staff got to the airport, they were able to make contact with all of the arriving campers except one. A 13-year-old young man named Travis. The staff checked the flight arrival board and confirmed that the plane Travis was supposed to have been on had indeed arrived. They then checked with the gate agent and asked for confirmation that Travis had traveled as an unattended minor on that flight. They were told no.

They called the camp director to advise him of the situation. The camp director then called Travis' parents, who confirmed that they had dropped him off at the airport, walked him through security, and saw him get on the plane, several hours earlier that day. So now what?

As it turns out, because this camp program was run identically on many different university campuses across the country, the parents believed that they had signed their child up to attend camp at a university in Florida, when actually their child had been registered in Ohio. Upon review of the camp's printed materials, one factor that the parents noted was that all of the locations were listed on all of the documentation. This scenario led the parents to believe, so they claimed, that once their child was registered into the program, he could simply show up and attend whatever campus location they chose.

In a way, that perception was true, because the same program was being offered at multiple campuses across the country. The communication breakdown seems to be in the follow-up documentation that was sent to the parents.

Lesson: Crystal clear communication and personal follow-up are essential. Much like what was discussed in Chapter 1, "Think Like a Parent," you need to look at your registration materials and your marketing media from an outsider's perspective. If anything appears unclear or is, in the slightest way, vague, it will be interpreted that way.

Follow-up is also critical. These parents were apparently told that all they needed to do was get their child on the plane and that their child would be met at the destination airport. Specific documentation and follow-up phone conversations, especially with out of state families who are not personally bringing their kids to camp, will go a long way toward removing any ambiguity in the course of making travel arrangements.

I'm Really Not a Fan

At the end of the very busy summer of camp, I called a friend of mine, who was a camp director in another state. She said, "So how was your summer?" I then replied, "Great. How was yours?"

She responded, "Oh my God, I am never hiring female British staff again." I replied: "No way! Me too. They all think they are the Queen or something." We then shared our mutual horror stories.

> *Disclaimer:* To all my English camp friends and colleagues,
>
> I'm sure that this situation is the exception, not the rule.

One summer, I worked at a very traditional camp. It had been run by the same family for generations. As such, it had separate dining rooms for the boys' camp and the girls' camp.

I noticed some strange behaviors from two of the female staff. One was not eating very much at each meal, while the other kept escalating her requests for special dietary needs, mind you that she did not indicate any dietary needs or allergies on her application.

The situation came to a head when the young woman who wasn't eating much actually fainted, while walking along the trail with a group of her cabinmates. We began to suspect an undiagnosed eating disorder. The other girl was also starting to eat less and less of the pre-planned camp menu food, choosing instead to eat only a very few bland items and some fruit.

The whole situation had me concerned that the overall health of these two female staff, but more importantly, for the message it was sending to our campers. Camp staff are often the ultimate role models for campers—old enough to be rock-star authorities and young enough to still be cool. The kids at both tables had already begun to emulate the actions and behaviors of their counselors.

The next morning, during our usual all-staff morning meeting, I asked a few very simple questions to the assembled group. "Is the job what you expected?" "Do any of you feel that you were misinformed or unprepared for the reality of the job?" "Do you feel misled in any way about what this job would be like?" "Do you have problems or concerns you'd like to address?"

After receiving nothing but positive comments and affirmations from the group and confirmation that everything was great, I said, "Then eat the food!" I then went on to inform them, as I had during staff training, that the campers idolize them. Their campers look up to them as role models. I told them that in the eyes of the campers, they can do no wrong. They are the camp heroes.

I told them that when a camper sees them turn their nose up at something on the menu, it gives them permission to do the same. When the campers see their hero cabin-counselor choose not to eat anything, they emulate that as well.

After the group meeting was over, I asked the two female counselors to stay back to have a more private conversation. I sat and spoke with each counselor, one at a time, and in the presence of another member of the administration staff.

To the girl who had taken to not eating at all and had fainted on the trail, we offered medical assistance. She refused, claiming that she was okay and promising to partake in all of the meals from that point on. We shared with her that her actions were posing a health risk to herself and her campers. We told her that if her campers emulate her behavior and begin becoming malnourished or dehydrated, it would become a liability risk for the camp. She said she understood.

We documented the conversation, as a written warning, and communicated to her that, should the situation continue, we would have to let her go. Often, in the case of international staff, employment termination would also void their tourist visa, and they would then be sent home to their home country immediately.

When we spoke to the other staffer, she said two phrases that I will never forget, probably because they were delivered with a British twist. About a few specific food items, she said; "I don't care for the texture." Furthermore, about the overall menu of the camp she said, "I'm really not a fan."

I showed her the description of the camp and the job description she read before she applied for the job at this camp. It very specifically states that traditional American camp fare will be served at meal times. I also pointed out to her that she participated in all of the meals during the staff-training week without issue. Finally, I shared her own application documents with her, in which she indicated that she had no special dietary needs, allergies, or other food requests.

Lesson: Be overly specific with the details of the job, your expectations, the realities of camp-life, sleeping areas, and especially meal service. You may even consider offering detailed descriptions of the actual menu that will be used at camp. Although I don't recommend it, I even know of a camp that sends photos of their menu items in the documents that they send to international staff applicants. You never want to put yourself in a position where a member of your camp staff will say, either "I didn't know," or "You didn't tell me."

The Runaway Kid

Cabin #3 was one camper short on their headcount, when the campers arrived for lunch on Thursday. It was quickly determined that while the group was getting ready in their cabin, this one boy had said something to the other campers about running away. Earlier, he had spoken with his cabin counselor about wanting to call home, and his counselor said he would make arrangements for that after lunch.

We believe that when all the campers were rounded up in the cabin to head for lunch, the camper in question had indeed left the property in an effort to return home. Subsequently, the cabin counselor noticed that the child was missing. He assumed that the camper had gone on ahead to the dining hall, and they would meet up there. Not the case.

When it was determined that the missing camper was not at lunch, and after speaking with the other campers in his cabin, we placed the camp on high alert. All available staff, not otherwise engaged in the direct supervision of campers, began searching the camp property, as well as the perimeter, for this child.

Because the camp is located adjacent to a community park, the park rangers were notified. They then sent patrols on the roads and adjoining trails, looking for the missing camper.

Following the emergency action plan of our camp, I called the parents of this camper. I told them that he had been missing for only about 20 minutes and that he had apparently communicated with other kids in his cabin of his desire to leave camp and head home. The parents said that they would immediately head toward camp. Fortunately, ours is more of an in-town facility, and the parents weren't far away. They actually discovered their child on their way to camp, walking on the sidewalk, heading in the opposite direction, about a half-mile from the camp entrance.

The parents called the camp, when they found their son, and drove him back onto the property. They then came to the camp office. They assured the camp director that they were very sorry and promised that their child wouldn't run away again. The camp director said that he too was very sorry about the situation and that the camper was not going to be allowed an opportunity to run away again, because he was not being admitted back into camp.

The camp director went on to describe the frenzied search and rescue operation that had begun and how the park rangers had been notified and had begun searching as well. At this point, the camper's mother again apologized and implored one more time that the camp director make an exception and let her child return to camp. Her request was denied.

A week later, the camp director received an email from the mother of this camper, requesting a refund and stating that her child was not allowed to participate in the full week of camp for which they had paid. The camp director then called her back and informed her of the camp's disciplinary policy, which included abusive behavior, fighting, and causing a disruption of camp programs. He also let her know that they had been about five minutes away from calling the sheriff's office, which would have resulted in her likely receiving a search and rescue bill for over $35,000. No refund was made.

Lesson: Double- and triple-check your written policies and all documentation that goes home to parents, especially anything that may result in a child being sent home from camp and/or anything that might generate a refund request.

Lost Luggage

In my second year of directing camp, I got a frantic walkie-talkie call on the first night of a session, from one of my cabin leaders. She could not find her camper's luggage, even after all of the lost luggage had been sorted. I took a quick look at the luggage bins and front gate, and then sent a sleeping bag, pillow, and some spare jammies out to the camper.

The next morning, I searched all of the camp, except of course, the cabin in which the camper was staying. I called the bus company, no luck. I eventually had to call the camper's mom, and though she was a bit upset, she understood. The cabin leaders picked up some more toiletries and clothes for the girl to help get her by, until her stuff was located or replacements could be sent from home.

That afternoon, I repeated my search all over the camp, looking under and behind everything. We made announcements at meals, and sent specialty staff on a hunt. I called the mom again to ask what she wanted to do.

It was decided that I would speak to the camper and see if she wanted to go home. As I drove up to the cabin, I saw a small green duffel-bag, slightly downhill from her cabin, so I picked it up and brought it in with me. Surprise!

It was the very bag in question. I called her mom again right away. Although she was grateful, she was also mad that it was in such an obvious place and had not previously been found.

Lesson: Trust, but verify. Don't take someone else's word for it, particularly if it's you who has to put your name on the line by calling a parent or making a drastic move. Chat with the "inconsolable" camper. Try your hand at the "impossible" activity. It's your word, and your camp's reputation at stake.

The Coolest Counselor

We used to have a contest called the "coolest counselor." This exercise involved an ice block and a tub of icy water. Staff would sit on the ice block and hold a bucket of ice in their lap during a super-hot August day. Then, they would sing camp songs.

Of course, the campers loved it, and the counselors were pumped to participate. We would time them and then rank who could sit on the ice the longest. It was completely a volunteer option, but, generally, something we had counselors lining up to do.

One year, we allowed a lead counselor to be in charge of this activity. Little did we know that he had also put salt in the bucket (in his mind, this step would make the ice colder and speed up the contest). Within 10 minutes of this process, a super competitive and tough counselor realized that something was wrong as she sat on the ice.

She then pulled the bucket off her lap and noticed that she had a very serious freeze-burn on her thighs. Unfortunately, she still has a small scar on her leg as a result of this situation. While we did not get sued, we could have been.

Lessons:
- That was a stupid contest to begin with and dangerous.
- Young people will literally do almost anything to win the contest and being named the "coolest counselor." The situation reinforced the fact that we need to be very careful, in every instance, to ensure that we are not putting the physical and emotional selves of our young counselors in harm's way.
- Whenever a staff member plans something, all details of the activity must be listed as to who, what, when, where, and how.
- Salt really does make ice a lot colder.

An Introduction to One Final Case History

One of the sessions that I occasionally teach at camp conferences is called, "Don't Panic!" It is generally offered to newer camp staff and covers a range of potentially uncomfortable things that they might encounter in a resident camp environment. We discuss everything, from first-aid and home-sickness issues all the way up to when campers or staff display possible eating disorders and the possibility that a camper might share some very uncomfortable or troubling news from home.

The worst-case scenario is when a camper becomes so comfortable and at ease with their cabin counselor over time, that they reveal some troubling or horrible detail about their home life. For example, neglect, sexual abuse, drug use, criminal behavior, etc.

The following case history went a little beyond what I usually prepare staff for during a typical training session.

Disclaimer: This one's a bit troubling. Read on at your own discretion.

Salad Therapy

I was volunteering at a Boy Scout summer camp for a few weeks one summer, serving as their camp commissioner and camp chaplain. In the world of Boy Scout summer camp, one of the staff leadership positions is that of "commissioner." The commissioner is basically the guest services person. He is the adult who goes around all day, every day, to make sure that all the campers are happy and that the scouts are getting into the merit badge classes they want, and so on. Because I also happen to be an ordained minister, I also provide campers with a friendly and safe place for them to share any of their personal concerns.

Early in the week, a scoutmaster pointed out to me a young man in his troop, named Jeff, whom he described as a bit troubled. I spoke with the boy a couple of times, just making random camp-conversation. My first instinct was that he was a little bit shy and possibly feeling homesick, in other words not much different from the 300 other kids at camp that week.

I made a point of spending at least one meal a day with his troop or in close proximity of his table, mostly to make him feel that he had a friend that he could rely on and reach out to, if he wanted to talk about anything. That was pretty much my typical mealtime routine anyway. The kitchen staff would tease me that I would never really eat during a meal, because I would spend the bulk of the time helicoptering around the dining hall to make sure everybody was happy. I would tell jokes or offer trivia mind-teasers. Whatever it took to keep the kids happy and engaged. This tactic on my part also allowed me to keep an eye on any specific campers whom I felt the need to watch out for or anyone who had been brought to my attention, like Jeff.

On the third day, after lunchtime, Jeff and I were walking outside the dining hall, and we went to sit on a picnic table. I asked him about his afternoon plans, and if he was enjoying camp this week. He said he had been having trouble sleeping. It was then that he shared with me that he was having some troubling thoughts that were keeping him awake. I said, "Like what?"

He sat there quietly for a while, thinking about how to tell me what he was thinking, then very quietly said to me, "I just can't stop thinking about what it would feel like to push a knife into my mom's neck." The way he said it was very matter-of-fact. No emotion, no anger or expressed hostility. It was as if he was wondering what it would feel like to ride a horse, shoot an arrow, or ask what's for dinner tonight. It was just one of the many curiosities in his life. It was spooky—except, that this one was keeping him up at night.

Well needless to say, this scenario was uncharted water for me. I'm a volunteer chaplain, not a psychiatrist. Another thing I noticed about Jeff was that when he spoke about hurting his mother, a kind of dark look came over his face. Not to make light of it, but it was almost like watching a horror movie. He could be laughing and joking around with his friends in the dining hall, and then it was almost like watching a shade get pulled down in front of his soul, as if a dark cloud was laid over him. If it was a horror movie, that's when the string bass and violas would start playing very low notes, and the hairs would stand up on the back of your neck.

So, after some very light prodding (e.g., asking him if he had those kind of thoughts about other people, if he had different thoughts about hurting his mother or if he were hearing voices telling him to do these things), I tried my best to shift the conversational topic.

For those concerned and as a side note, I did speak with Jeff's scoutmaster. Treading very lightly and not wanting to divulge personal information, I simply asked the scoutmaster if he knew about some of the specifics that were troubling Jeff. He said very bluntly, "You mean the way he thinks about hurting his mom?"

I was a little surprised to learn that it was kind of public knowledge, albeit within a small circle. The scoutmaster told me that he had been in communication with Jeff's father, that this was an ongoing issue, and that Jeff was in therapy.

So okay, now they sent him with me to talk about all this. In hindsight, I get the feeling they were using me just as a way to give themselves a break and to allow them to focus some attention on some of the other scouts in their group. Not a choice that I think I would've made. On the other hand, there we were. So be it.

Jeff and I began to discuss ways to take his mind off the topic of violent thoughts about his mother. Together, we created salad therapy.

One of the things that we would do together was to walk around camp and talk, quite honestly in my attempt to get him to think about something else. During one of these talk-and-walk sessions, we walked through the dining hall, just as the kitchen staff was preparing to layout dinner service. The staff had just finished setting up a very impressive salad bar, and Jeff and I began talking about what he likes in his salad.

The kitchen staff let us hit the food a little early and allowed us each to make a salad. We started with the big bowl of mixed lettuce. I pointed to it and said, "Do you like all the stuff in there?" He responded, "Yeah, pretty much, but not that purple stuff," referring to the pieces of red cabbage.

At that point, we worked our way down the salad bar together. The subsequent conversation went something like this: "So what else do you like in your salad? Do you like those little tomatoes?" "Yeah, they're okay." "How about those cucumber slices?" "Yeah, those too." "How about those little mini corn-on-the-cob things and the black olives?" "Ewww. Those are gross!" "Cottage cheese?" "Boo!" "Sliced peaches?" "Oh yeah! Those are really good!"

Then, we moved down to dressings. "So what kind of salad dressing do you put on your salad? I use Italian." He said, "Yeah, that's my favorite too." "How about ranch?" "I dip my pizza in that sometimes, but I don't put it on my salad." "What about blue cheese?" "Gross!"

Finally, we passed by the toppings section. I said, "Okay, now for the good stuff! Bacon bits?" "Oh yeah!" "Sesame seeds?" "They're okay, I guess." Good times, oh yeah, cruising the salad bar for sure!

We then grabbed a seat at the end of the dining hall and talked about our salads. I suggested that every time his mind wandered, and he began to find himself having negative feelings about his mom, I wanted him to think about salad. He said okay. As we finished eating, we discussed other things, like how much he enjoyed canoeing and the archery range, and if he was going to participate in a skit at the closing campfire.

The rest of the day went pretty much without incident. When I saw him at breakfast the next morning, he seemed like every other kid in the camp. He appeared happy to be there and said he was looking forward to a good day.

About a half hour later, I was standing out by the flagpole, talking to some of the camp staff. When breakfast ended, and all the scouts came out of the dining hall, I saw Jeff coming out with his group, and he had that dark look on his face.

I shouted over to him and waved, "Hey Jeff." He looked at me, but didn't verbally respond. I then shouted, "Black olives?!" His face immediately lit up, and he yelled back, "Gross!"

I gave him a thumbs-up and said, "Keep thinking salad." He returned the thumbs-up, and shouted, "OK." He then walked off with the rest of his group. When he was almost out of sight, I shouted, "Blue cheese!" Then, came his echoing reply, "Gross!"

That evening was the closing campfire and there was no additional incident or issues with Jeff. The next morning, anticipating the long drive home, his troop packed up and left early. I did not get the chance to say goodbye. I never found out what happened to Jeff. I hope that the therapy his scoutmaster said he was getting has done him some good and that he grows to become a happy, well-adjusted person.

Lesson: Don't panic—uncomfortable situations arise. Deal with them as best you can. – Furthermore, be aware of the fact that you may never know the final outcome of a situation. That's okay, too.

Surprise Ending

I know that I said that salad therapy was the last case study, but I wanted to close this chapter on more of a high note. Accordingly, allow me to introduce you to Mateo. His is the feel-good camp story of my lifetime ... so far.

Secret Super Powers

Young Mateo was an eight-year-old camper, attending a week-long resident camp program (a rental-group event), as a camper with the Muscular Dystrophy Association (MDA). Every child attending this camp was afflicted with muscular dystrophy. Each camper was at a different stage of the disease, however. Early-stage kids were pretty mobile, needing only some basic crutches and sometimes leg-braces. Mid-stage kids were in wheelchairs, while advance-stage kids were completely immobile and traveled in fully automated electric chairs, often with the need for head and next support.

The theme for the week was Super Heroes. As a result, all of the camp counselors, personal aides, and staff were dressed in a colorful variety of Superman, Batman, and Wonder Woman outfits, as well as a few outfits I've never seen before.

During the opening ceremony, each camper was instructed to select their own personal superpower. They were told that they could share the secret with their camp counselor, but not to tell anybody else. The underlying premise was that at the end of the week, during the closing campfire, everyone's secret superpowers would be revealed. At various times during the week, different things would happen that would allow the campers to try to guess each other's secret superpower. They would then write notes about each other and put them in a big box on the main stage.

Anticipating the arrival of this group, we had modified our zip line area several months earlier to accommodate limited mobility and wheelchair-bound campers. Thursday morning had been designated as the time that these kids would go up to the zip line. Accordingly, after breakfast, everyone headed in that direction.

As you might imagine, it took up the pretty much the whole day to get this group through the activity. Just the process of getting everyone into a safety harness took at least five times longer than usual. When it was finally Mateo's turn, he worked his way up to the front of the line and onto the zip-launching platform. He would keep his leg braces on for his trip down the zip line, but would need to turn over his crutches to his camp facilitator.

Once the safety tether was attached to Mateo's harness, a very strange look came across his face. It's not unusual for kids, and adults, to feel fear right before going down the zip line. The look on Mateo's face was different. He looked concerned and worried. His camp facilitator then walked over and asked him if anything was wrong. Mateo replied, "My secret super power is flying, but now it won't be a secret anymore."

A feeling of relief, goose bumps, and a "down-to-our-soul," feeling that this setting was a prime example of why we were all proud to be part of the camp experience came across everyone there. Even the volunteer firefighters who had come to help the kids that day were crying.

Mateo soared across the canyon, if only for a few seconds; free from the gravity he had spent most of his young life fighting. He wore a smile on his face like no other. All of the assembled campers, staff, and volunteers cheered, like he had just scored the winning touchdown of the Superbowl.

There was not a dry eye in the house, as we were all filled with an extreme sense of purpose and clarity. In that moment, we were one—one family, one community, one super hero fan club.

Camp

We don't do it for the income
We do it for the outcome!

9

Closing Campfire

This book is by no means the end-all of everything you might encounter in your camp career, but it's a start. I encourage to you be open and communicative with your staff, your vendors, your business allies, and your customers.

One of the most amazing benefits that we all have as members of the greater camp community is each other and a connection to the American Camp Association (ACA)—your first and best resources. The ACA is a community of camp professionals who, for over 100 years, have joined together to share knowledge and experience and to ensure the quality of camp programs. Because of the diverse 9,000 plus membership and exceptional programs, children and adults have the opportunity to learn powerful lessons in community, character building, skill development, and healthy living—lessons that cannot be learned anywhere else.

As a leading authority in youth development, the ACA works to preserve, promote, and improve the camp experience. Our association is committed to helping our members and all camps provide the following:

- Camp communities committed to a safe, nurturing environment
- Caring, competent adult role models
- Healthy, developmentally appropriate experiences
- Service to the community and the natural world
- Opportunities for leadership and personal growth
- Discovery, experiential education, and learning opportunities
- Excellence and continuous self-improvement

Resource file: www.acacamps.org/about/who-we-are

I encourage you to connect with your fellow camp professionals. Introduce yourself, trade contact information, make phone calls, and send emails. I have yet to reach out to this amazing community and not receive immediate and valuable assistance. Chances are, whatever challenge you are having, there's someone out there who's been down that road already and would be more than happy to share their experiences and solution(s) with you.

If, after reading this book, you still need help, please visit my website at:

www.michaeljacobus.com

My sincere thanks to the many camp directors who contributed to the case studies section. You guys are truly rock stars!

My Camp Biography

I'm a life-long camp enthusiast, beginning in first grade when I went to Camp Lodestar for the first time. The following is a short list of my crazy camp background. (How many camp-jobs have you had?):

❑ Positions:

- Camper
- Cub Scout
- C.I.T.
- Boy Scout
- Jr. Counselor
- Eagle Scout
- Sr. Counselor
- Head Counselor
- Den Leader
- Cub Scoutmaster
- Scoutmaster
- Program Coordinator
- Cub Scout Committee Chairman
- Camp Commissioner
- Vochele (South Africa)
- Camp Director
- Session Speaker
- LCOL Membership Chair
- Associate Visitor
- Lead Visitor
- LCOL Standards Committee
- National Standards Commission
- Standards Instructor

❑ Recognitions

- ACA Program Excellence
- Excellence in Sustainability Education (BSA)
- ACA Excellence in Standards

❑ Favorite Camp Things:

(Sung to "My Favorite Things"—from The Sound of Music)

*Unclogging toilets
and fixing sunglasses.
ATM trips
and payroll advances.
Drying the tears
of counselors and kids.
Calling suppliers
and getting low bids!*

*S'mores at the creek
and camper-stew too.
Hoping that sniffly kid
has not the flu.
Planning events
and inflating balls.
Answering every
last parent's phone calls!*

*Sketchy bandwidth,
counselor days off,
Kids who say they're ill.
I simply keep smiling
even though it's compiling,
Remembering camp's a thrill.*

*Food allergies
and letters from home.
Keeping an eye
on campers who roam.
Resetting mousetraps
and fixing the holes.
What'll come next,
nobody knows!*

*Teenage romances
and kids who are homesick.
Siesta-time
and watching a card-trick.
Singing to cookies
who make all the food.
Wondering why that kid
calls me "dude."*

*Sketchy bandwidth,
counselor days off,
kids who say they're ill.
I simply keep smiling,
even though it's compiling,
Remembering camp's a thrill.*

ABOUT THE AUTHOR

Michael Jacobus is a nationally recognized camp professional and frequent presenter at camp conferences and retreats. He has an extensive background in youth development, staff training, operations, and outdoor education. Michael has worked with private, public, and nonprofit groups including: the American Camp Association (ACA), Disney, the Boy Scouts of America (BSA), National Geographic, the Red Cross, Global Camps Africa, the Muscular Dystrophy Association, Nature Partners, Green Camps Initiative, and the National Science Teachers Association.

He has been honored with the national award for Excellence in Sustainability Education from the BSA and has been recognized for Program Excellence and Excellence in Standards by the ACA.

Michael is an Eagle Scout who has drawn from a diverse background of experiences to become a dynamic industry leader. He has spent time as a ship captain on Lake Tahoe, a radio personality, pastor, magazine publisher, food broker & chemist. He's owned a screen-print & embroidery shop, designed two frisbee golf courses, and taught drama, improv theatre, and stagecraft at the elementary and university level. When he finds the time, he occasionally performs as an opera singer (tenor / baritone), most recently singing at Christmastime as a member of the Disneyland Candlelight Choir.